your time-starved marriage

how to stay connected at the speed of life

Resources by Les & Leslie Parrott

Books

51 Creative Ideas for Marriage Mentors
Becoming Soul Mates
The Complete Guide to Marriage Mentoring
Getting Ready for the Wedding
I Love You More (and workbooks)
Just the Two of Us
Love Is . . .
The Love List
Love Talk (and workbooks)
The Marriage Mentor Training Manual (for Husbands/Wives)
Meditations on Proverbs for Couples
Pillow Talk
Questions Couples Ask
Relationships (and workbook)
Saving Your Marriage Before It Starts (and workbooks)
Saving Your Second Marriage Before It Starts (and workbooks)

Video Curriculum — ZondervanGroupware®

I Love You More
Love Talk
The Complete Resource Kit for Marriage Mentoring
Relationships
Saving Your Marriage Before It Starts

Audio Pages®

Love Talk
Relationships
Saving Your Marriage Before It Starts
Saving Your Second Marriage Before It Starts

Books by Les Parrott

The Control Freak
Helping Your Struggling Teenager
High Maintenance Relationships
The Life You Want Your Kids to Live
Seven Secrets of a Healthy Dating Relationship
Shoulda, Coulda, Woulda
Once Upon a Family
25 Ways to Win with People (coauthored with John Maxwell)
Love the Life You Live (coauthored with Neil Clark Warren)

Books by Leslie Parrott

If You Ever Needed Friends, It's Now
You Matter More Than You Think
God Loves You Nose to Toes (children's book)
Marshmallow Clouds (children's book)

your time-starved marriage

how to stay connected at the speed of life

Drs. Les & Leslie Parrott

Authors of *Saving Your Marriage Before It Starts*

ZONDERVAN®

GRAND RAPIDS, MICHIGAN 49530 USA

ZONDERVAN.COM/
AUTHORTRACKER

ZONDERVAN®

Your Time-Starved Marriage
Copyright © 2006 by Les & Leslie Parrott

This title is also available as a Zondervan audio product.
Visit www.zondervan.com/audiopages for more information.

Requests for information should be addressed to:
Zondervan, *Grand Rapids, Michigan 49530*

Library of Congress Cataloging-in-Publication Data

Parrott, Les.
    Your time-starved marriage : how to stay connected at the speed of life / Les &
Leslie Parrott.
       p. cm.
    Includes bibliographical references.
    ISBN-13: 978-0-310-24597-1
    ISBN-10: 0-310-24597-4
    1. Married people—Time management. 2. Marriage. I. Parrott, Leslie L., 1964–
II. Title.
HQ734.P22 2006
646.7'8—dc22
                                        2005033436

This edition printed on acid-free paper.

Published in association with Yates & Yates, LLP, Attorneys and Counselors, Suite 1000, Literary Agent, Orange, CA.

Interior design by Michelle Espinoza

Printed in the United States of America

---

06 07 08 09 10 11 12 • 18 17 16 15 14 13 12 11 10 9 8 7 6 5 4 3

To Todd and K. K. Parmenter

*A couple who has been an inspiration and gift to us
in our own efforts to reclaim moments together.
May your marriage grow sweeter and sweeter as time goes by.*

- Are you feeling overscheduled and underconnected?
- Would you like to know your unique "time style"—as well as your spouse's?
- Are you looking for the secret to recouping the rest and recreation you crave?
- Do you want to find a surefire way to create more meaningful time together each day?

If so, you're ready to reclaim the moments you've been missing together. You're ready to feed your time-starved marriage.

contents

acknowledgments

We are profoundly grateful to ...

Our Zondervan team. You caught our vision for this message the second we shared it. Thanks for helping us help time-starved couples.

Janice Lundquist. You are our number one "time maker" and we simply can't say thanks enough for the gift of your time to our lives.

Sealy Yates. Your wisdom and guidance on this project is beyond compare. And, personally, time with you is always well spent.

Kevin Small. Your genius of rethinking how to maximize our message to time-starved couples is forever valued, as is your friendship.

this better be quick

We have so much time and so little to do.
Strike that, reverse it.
Roald Dahl

If you're like us, you're prone to skip the preface of some books — to save a little time. After all, why mess with a lengthy introduction when your day is already too full, schedules too compact, time too precious.

So if you're inclined to forgo the appetizer and get straight to the main course of a book on maximizing your time together, we don't want to slow you down. We're just as eager as you are to get to the good stuff.

Allow us simply to say at the outset that we have deliberately designed this book for a couple on the go. We wanted to be concise and to the point, so that each chapter could be read through easily in a single sitting. You won't be wading through redundancies or elaborate filler to find the bottom line on what you can do — starting today — to reclaim the moments you've been missing together.

Les and Leslie Parrott
Seattle, Washington

a quick overview

Part 1 of the book sets the stage for a couple to find a new relationship with time. It reveals the two lies that every time-starved couple buys into, and it shows you how to conquer the archenemy of every relationship—busyness.

Part 2 starts off by showing how you, personally, approach time. Chances are that you handle time quite differently from your spouse. We'll also give you a step-by-step approach to making more time together and maximizing the moments that matter most. And we'll wrap up this section by helping you hunt down and smoke out the time bandits that will forever stalk your relationship if not captured.

Part 3 delves into three specific areas where you are most likely to reclaim meaningful moments you've been missing out on: mealtime, money time, and leisure time. Once you get a lock on these three areas, you'll be shocked to see all the free time you've been leaving on the table—sometimes literally.

At the end of each chapter, you will find reflection questions. Guaranteed to take only a few minutes, these exercises are expressly designed to help you apply the chapter to your relationship.

Each chapter also ends with a reference to a workbook exercise. If you are looking for a fun way to apply the ideas of this book to your marriage, we invite you to use the separate booklet called *Your Time-Starved Marriage Workbook*. We suggest that you buy one workbook for each of you so that you both have space to write—and so your answers don't influence each other before you talk about them together.[1]

Your Time-Starved Marriage Workbook also contains a section for small group study. Discussing the material in a small group can be an invaluable way to learn the principles and practices taught in this book. In addition, we have developed a six-session DVD curriculum of *Your Time-Starved Marriage* that's specially designed for use with small groups, though feel free to use it as a couple if you and your partner prefer to go through the questions on your own or are unable to connect with others who are studying the same curriculum. You can learn more about the DVD and the workbooks at your local bookstore or at *www.RealRelationships.com*.

part 1

loving on borrowed time

"Most new books are forgotten within a year," said Evan Esar, "especially by those who borrow them." Well, whether you bought or borrowed the book you're holding, we want you to remember and practice its principles for far more than a year. Truly, we believe that what you are about to learn can change the course of your relationship forever.

You see, most married couples live and love on borrowed time. They spend their prime time on everything "out there," and then scrape together whatever is left over and bank on the time they're borrowing from the future—saying *someday* we'll do this or that, *tomorrow* we won't be so busy, *eventually* things will be different. But will they? Really?

There's a better way. To quote Shakespeare, "Neither a borrower nor a lender be ... borrowing dulls the edge of husbandry." So learn how to live free and clear of your time debt and own outright each moment you have together.

1

anybody have the time?

Time isn't a commodity, something you pass around like cake.
Time is the substance of life.
Antoinette Bosco

Time may not be a commodity, but it is every couple's most valuable resource. Whatever financial or material resources you have stockpiled, they don't hold a candle to time. And if you are burning your proverbial candle at both ends, you know exactly what we mean.

In these hectic, hurry-up, stressful times, every couple we know — including ourselves — is rushing around to get more done in less time. Ironically, that's exactly what we end up with: less time. So we jump back onto the treadmill for fear of losing ground.

However, in the rat race to get ahead, or just to keep up, we too often neglect what makes life worth living: our relationships — especially our marriage. Life in the fast lane inevitably means less time with the one you love. Where does time go? We try to make it, save it, seize it, buy it, and borrow it. We even try to "steal" it. And yet time continues to elude us.

Traveling at the Speed of Life

After resolving communication meltdowns, most couples report that finding time together is their top relational need. And yet there is precious little written about finding time for each other. When we decided to explore this subject for our own relationship, we couldn't find a single book on the topic. Not one.

We found plenty of books for couples on communication, a plethora of resources on sex, and an overabundance on money management. But not a peep of help on how couples can better manage their time together. Stephan Rechtschaffen, author of *Timeshifting*, must have been right when he said, "We think much more about the use of our money, which is renewable, than we do about the use of our time, which is irreplaceable."[1]

Strange, isn't it? The moments we miss together as a couple are gone forever. Irreplaceable. And yet, until now, there has not been a single book for couples on how to better manage this priceless resource. That's what compelled us to write this book. As a married couple, we are determined to take back the time we've been missing together and maximize the moments we have. Since you're reading this book, we know you probably feel the same way.

In fact, we urge you, right now, to consider what your life together would look like if time was on your side — if you managed your time more than it managed you. Be as concrete as you can but don't talk about how your schedules might change. That typically turns into a gripe session. Instead, focus on what the emotional and relational consequences would be for each of you if you were to slay the busyness monster and have the kind of time together you long for. In other words, how will you know when you are maximizing your moments together?

> *When Solomon said there was a time and a place for everything, he had not encountered the problem of parking his automobile.*
>
> **Bob Edwards**

The Question

Mario and Melissa, living in the fast lane and dangerously close to a collision, came to see us for counseling. "We feel like strangers," they told us. "We share the same address and sleep in the same bed, but our relationship has become nothing more than a pit stop with a dried-up fuel pump."

Mario and Melissa were running on empty, and they knew it. The consequence? On the one hand, Melissa felt isolated and alone and would often say, "I feel like I'm on my own. Mario gets impatient and short with me these days, and it makes me withdraw."

Mario, on the other hand, felt burdened and sometimes nagged. He'd tell us, "Melissa doesn't understand the pressure I'm under at work, and so I've quit talking about it."

They squabbled for a while about balancing child care while working, and they whined and complained about not having enough time. But before the conversation escalated, we intervened by asking the question, "How will you know when you are maximizing your moments together?" The room fell silent. We handed each of them a pencil and paper and asked them to write their answer.

"I don't need to write it," Mario said as he set the paper aside. "I already have the answer: We'll be maximizing our moments together when we both feel understood and like we're on each other's team."

Melissa agreed. "That's right ... like we used to be before life got so busy."

We spent the next few minutes making their answer more concrete. We challenged them to identify specific times when they last felt this way. We talked about how and when these times happened. They both agreed the experience had to do with feeling fully present and invested in each other. They didn't want to feel judged or lay blame. They wanted to play tennis together again, laugh more, and enjoy each other's company.

The very process of discussing the positive outcome of maximizing their time seemed to make it more within reach. So why don't you take a moment, right now, to do the same. Get concrete about what your life together would be like if you were maximizing your moments. This will ensure that you get the most out of this book.

> *By the time we've reached the w of now the n is ancient history.*
>
> **Michael Frayn**

The more specific you can be, the better. And consider your answer a work in progress. You'll fine-tune it as we move through the next few chapters.

Don't Be Scared

That being said, we want to clear up any potential for unnecessary anxiety or misunderstanding right at the start. This is not a book about being more productive — it's a book about being more connected. And it's not a book about going back in time to an idealized, preindustrial era where a slower pace romantically resolved all ills for couples. This is a book about real life in the real world. It's written by a busy couple with two little kids, by frequent flyers who speed-dial our cell phones, instant message, drive in the express lane, and juggle schedules. In other words, if you have an unspoken fear that we are going to ask you to do something radical and short-change your productivity in the process ... and then make you feel guilty if you don't, you can relax. We just want to help you be more connected with each other as you're traveling at the speed of life.

part 1: loving on borrowed time

And we could not be more excited to share with you the secrets we've learned about doing just that. After scouring numerous studies, interviewing experts, and experimenting with techniques, we believe we have developed a program that will allow you to reclaim the moments you've been missing together. Whether you're running at a breathless rate, living on the edge of exhaustion, or simply looking for new and practical ways to stay connected, we want to give you the tools for feeding your time-starved relationship and maximizing each moment you have.

> *Life moves pretty fast. If you don't stop to enjoy it sometimes, it will pass you by.*
>
> **Ferris Bueller**

For Reflection

1. Do you know the experience of rushing around to get more done more quickly only to find that you seem to have less time on your hands? If so, why do you think this is so?
2. Little has been written about how to manage time as a married couple. Do you have any hunches as to why? What's the best advice on time management that you've ever received as a couple?
3. How will you know when you are maximizing your moments together? Be specific and concrete.

Workbook Exercise:
Maximizing Your Time Quotient

Both you and your spouse can find this optional workbook exercise in *Your Time-Starved Marriage Workbook* (*for Men/for Women*). Workbooks are available separately at your local bookstore or online at *www.RealRelationships.com*.

To maximize your time quotient, this workbook exercise will use a pie chart to help you determine more precisely where and how you are currently using your time. You will also pinpoint how much time you are spending together and how you would most like to spend this time.

2

is your marriage slipping into the future?

Love must be fed and nurtured . . .
first and foremost it demands time.
David Mace

In 1973, a song by Jim Croce plinked out on nearly every radio station in the country. "Time in a Bottle" was the number-one hit that autumn. In the song, Jim spoke of wanting to make the days he had with his wife last forever. And his haunting chorus reminded us that there "never seems to be enough time" with the one you love.

The personal poignancy of Croce's song could have never been predicted upon its release. Just days later, on September 20, 1973, Jim Croce's light aircraft was taking off from a small airstrip in Natchitoches, Louisiana, when the plane snagged a treetop at the end of the dim runway, sending Jim and five others to their deaths.

Jim's wife, Ingrid, was left with only their infant son, who was half-blind, and the heartbreaking legacy of a song she must have heard nearly everywhere she turned that year and every year since. Today, Ingrid owns a restaurant in San Diego, called Croce's, where a giant mural portrait of Jim takes up the back wall. "It serves as an inspiration to me," Ingrid once told a reporter, "to remember how fragile life is and to never ever take for granted the time we have with the one we love."

> *Guard well your spare moments. They are like uncut diamonds. Discard them and their value will never be known. Improve them and they will become the brightest gems in a useful life.*
>
> Ralph Waldo Emerson

Many of Jim Croce's songs touched on our feeble attempts to reach back and grasp at a past that has already slipped away. "Operator" and "I Got a Name" are two that easily come to mind. In his brief, thirty-year life, Jim Croce already had a handle on the significance of time and its tenuous relationship to marriage.

And chances are that you, too, are well aware of the fleeting nature of time. We all know that time passes too quickly. If we could save time in a bottle, there's little doubt what we would do with it. And yet, the time we do have—the precious time that is given to us each day—is too often frittered away.

Preparing for a Time That's Already Here

Why does it seem we squander the very thing we want to save? Because, more often than not, we are so busy preparing for the future that we miss out on the moment at hand. We realized that truth early in our marriage.

When we were both in graduate school and newly married, we lived in a tiny apartment in Southern California. Tucked into the corner of our main room, actually the *only* room, was a desk and a computer where we spent an inordinate amount of time. Day or night, it seemed one of us was on that computer working away at a term paper or dissertation. And taped to the top edge of the computer screen was a small piece of paper containing a quote from Abraham Maslow. We placed it in this prominent position where we would see it every day.

It read:

> Some people spend their entire lives indefinitely preparing
> to live.

Why this quote? Because Leslie and I were beginning six long years of demanding graduate work, and we knew we were vulnerable to a deadly trap: putting life on hold until the grueling task was finished. "Once we graduate ..." was a tempting refrain. "Once we graduate, we'll take a vacation ... we'll have time to take walks ... we'll eat better ... we'll focus on our relationship ... we'll enjoy life." Of course, you don't have to be working at a PhD to be swindled by this empty promise.

After our graduation, the temptation simply evolved: "Once we get a job" or "Once we pay off our student loans" or "Once we buy a house." You get the idea. Like every other couple, we were susceptible to spending our married lives indefinitely preparing to live. We've all been there. If you're honest, you've been tempted to put life on hold, to put off enjoying time together, because an important milestone was standing in your way. Or maybe it still is. Do any of these phrases sound familiar?

Once the kids are older ...

Once I get my raise ...

Once we get a new house ...

Once I quit my job ...

Or if you haven't put life on hold as you're preparing to live it, maybe you've found yourself on the proverbial "Someday Isle" — a euphemism for the tropical vacation that never materializes. "Someday, I'll have more free time." "Someday, I'll take you on a great trip." "Someday, I'll build that porch we've always wanted." "Someday ..."

It's been said that the saddest word in our language is *some-day*. Why? Because *someday* eventually turns into "if only." And "if onlys" are the result of time you can't recoup: "If only we would have made more free time." "If only we would have taken that trip." "If only we would have built that porch." "If only . . ."

It's at that moment — when "someday" becomes "if only" — that your marriage slips quietly into the future, and you wonder how you could have let that happen. How could you have taken time — not to mention your relationship — for granted?

Don't say you don't have enough time. You have exactly the same number of hours per day that were given to Helen Keller, Michelangelo, Mother Teresa, Leonardo da Vinci, Thomas Jefferson, and Albert Einstein.

H. Jackson Brown Jr.

Perhaps nothing else distinguishes the most fulfilled and happy couples as much as their tender loving care of time. They spend it wisely. Seeing the value of their times together, they are determined to guard against wasting them. They know that each moment, no matter how fleeting, holds value for them as a couple, and they prize the opportunity to make the most out of it. They understand what so many couples don't: that only time affords the luxury of creating memories to be cherished. And they are bent on racking up as many memories as possible.

The Test of Time

The first step in reclaiming your time as a couple is to realize that your life is happening now. Not someday. Not once something else is achieved or a certain phase has passed. It's happening today. This is it. Now.

This seemingly obvious fact is never quite realized by couples in a time-starved marriage. They believe real life is just around the corner; it's almost here, but not quite yet. They live in a deluded state that is characterized by two lies: (1) time can be stopped and (2) time can be saved. Dangling these two erroneous beliefs in front of us is time's test for every couple. If we swallow them whole, we fail the test. If we see their absurdity, we succeed. Let's take a quick look at each.

Myth 1: Time Can Be Stopped

"Time marches on." Ever heard that expression? Well, it's never uttered in the time-starved marriage. These couples are convinced they can press the pause button on life. Not literally, of course, but relationally and emotionally. For example, they believe they can freeze-frame their marriage at a

> *There is never enough time, unless you're serving it.*
>
> **Malcolm Forbes**

particularly romantic period—not realizing that love is fluid, like a stream you can never jump into at the exact same place.

Or they view their love like a rosebush, thinking it will always be in bloom, and then they're shocked to find the flowers withering on the stem. They haven't come to the realization that love, true love that goes the distance, changes. It has seasons.

Or these couples may try to stop time because a major project, a looming goal, or a prolonged assignment demands they put their relationship on hold. But again, they can't reenter it a week, a month, or a year later, just where they left off. Time marches on.

Some time ago, the commanding officer of the Second Battalion Marines, now the most decorated battalion in US history, called us from Iraq and asked if we would be willing to speak to his returning soldiers about how to reenter life at home. We gladly accepted the invitation. And the thrust of our message to these valiant men and women at Camp Pendleton had to do with realizing that the person you haven't seen for six months is not the same person you said good-bye to half a year earlier. Whether they were soldiers on the battlefield or spouses on the home front, they have changed. And it's your job as a couple, we told them, to get reacquainted. Life has changed. You both have changed. And if your expectations don't change accordingly, you are in for a very rocky homecoming.

Whatever the circumstances, couples who don't understand this fundamental fact inevitably utter the worn-out excuse: "We've grown apart." Truth is, couples don't grow apart. They simply grow, and they either choose to make space in this growth for each other or not. Individuals change, interests evolve, opportunities appear, or a crisis happens. The passage of time guarantees change. And you can't stop time.

Myth 2: Time Can Be Saved

A *USA Today* poll asked a group of mothers what they needed most. The most popular response was: "More time in the day." Money was fourth on the list after patience and respect.[1] Makes perfect sense. The mothers chose as their most needed entity the one thing that's finite. After all, there are ways to make more money. And you can cultivate character qualities like patience. You can even do things to gain another's respect. But you can't have more time. As Queen Elizabeth I said, "I'd give all my possessions for a moment of time."

Nobody, no matter how wealthy or influential, gets more minutes in his or her day. Each and every one of us has the same 1,440 minutes each and every day. Once those minutes have passed, that's it. You can't retrieve them. You can't borrow against them, and you certainly can't save some of them for another day. Time is non-renewable; not one minute of our lives can be placed in abeyance or lived more than once.

But this fact doesn't stop some time-starved couples from trying. They are under the false impression that if they work hard now they'll accumulate more "marriage time" later. But life doesn't work that way. The time we "save" is inevitably consumed by more work. And love doesn't work that way either. You can't save up moments to be more connected and then cash them in when the time is right.

> *Time slides through our fingers like a well-greased string.*
>
> **James Dobson**

That's about as absurd as thinking you can go without food or sleep for a couple weeks and then catch up on your eating and sleeping when you have "more time." A body needs to be nourished daily. So does a marriage. Not until you accept this fact will you relinquish your vain attempts to save up time for romantic moments when they'll fit more easily into your hectic schedule.

Time Well Spent

A couple years ago, we wrote a little book called *The Love List*. It's a simple plan for nourishing your marriage. In it, we say a couple should do two things every day in their marriage, two things every week, two things every month, and two things every year. One of those things we say a couple should do every day is to find something that makes them both laugh. We talk about how to study your spouse's funny bone and daily bring doses of humor into your relationship.

We can't begin to tell you the number of grateful readers who have emailed us with stories of how this simple advice has helped them. "We've always had a pretty good marriage," Lisa wrote, "but when we began to follow your Love List and treat laughter as our daily vitamin, it brought our relationship to a new level." Lisa went on to tell us how they had made it a contest to see who could find the funniest joke or comic or picture or whatever to make the other person laugh each day. "We used to go through the motions at the end of our weary workday, but now we are laughing all the way to the kitchen table each night before dinner. It's redefined our relationship."

How you spend your time has a way of doing that. Every moment in time offers a choice. You are free to spend your moments laughing or not laughing. Poet Carl Sandburg put it this way: "Time is the most valuable coin in your life. You and you alone will determine how that coin will be spent."

Are you spending your moments in ways that will return big dividends, or are your valuable moments dribbling away without notice? How you choose to spend your time reveals more about you than nearly anything else. In fact, how you spend your time not only defines you, it defines your marriage. How much time you choose to spend together and how you choose to spend it reveals the value of your relationship. If you're spending your time wisely, the value of your marriage increases. If not, you're not only wasting your time, but your marriage as well.

In *The Time Bind*, Arlie Hochschild studies a Fortune 500 company and finds a surprising trend: despite family-friendly policies in the workplace, employees are opting to spend more, not less, time in the office.[2] Over the past two decades, the average worker has lengthened his or her work schedule by 164 hours every year of work and shortened vacation time by 14 percent. Most employees didn't even use all their vacation days.

Hochschild asserts that Americans are not working overtime because of money or a fear of layoffs. Instead, the average worker doesn't mind that work is eroding time at home. Apparently, somewhere in between "Have a good day, dear" and "Honey, I'm home," there has been a role reversal between home and work. Thanks to twentieth-century concepts such as company spirit and loyalty, the workplace is becoming increasingly cozy and comfortable, while home, with its diapers and dirty dishes, is seen as harried and hectic. One interviewee tells Hochschild, "I come to work to relax."

If this sentiment hits a little too close to home, literally, it's time to reclaim what you've been missing. It's time to rediscover your greatest refuge: home.

Time Is What You Make It

I (Leslie) learned a big lesson about a decade ago. The phone was always ringing on Sunday afternoons when I had planned to relax and recharge my batteries. I'd answer and then feel agitated and irritable with the person who'd called. Les said to me one Sunday, "If you don't want to talk, why do you keep picking up the phone?" Aha moment: Just because the phone is ringing doesn't mean I have to respond.

> *Dost thou love life? Then do not squander time, for that is the stuff life is made of.*
>
> **Benjamin Franklin**

We all control what we do with our time. Even when it seems out of control, we're still in control. Our choices, from moment to moment, are the rudder that directs where we go and what we do.

A reporter once asked President Theodore Roosevelt with whom he most enjoyed spending his time. The president responded that he would rather spend time with his wife than with any of the world's notables. Roosevelt understood what every time-starved couple needs to learn: Time is what you make it. And each of the following chapters of this book are going to show you exactly how to make the most of it.

For Reflection

1. In what ways have you spent your life "indefinitely preparing to live"? In other words, when have you more or less put your life on hold until a specific milestone was met? If you could do it over again, how might you do it differently?

2. As you review your past week, what choices have you made to maximize your time in ways that are meaningful (not necessarily productive) to you?

Workbook Exercise:
Is Your Marriage Slipping into the Future?

Both you and your spouse can find this optional workbook exercise in *Your Time-Starved Marriage Workbook* (*for Men/for Women*). Workbooks are available separately at your local bookstore or online at *www.RealRelationships.com*.

Ever feel like you need an alarm clock to wake you out of your mundane marriage routines? Let's face it, sometimes our marriage moments slip right past us because we approach our days in zombie-like fashion, never really awake to the potential of how a routine moment could be so much more. The exercise in the accompanying workbook will help you wake up and put new life back into your relationship. It will help you prevent your relationship from slipping into the future.

---

busyness: the archenemy
of every marriage

For fast-acting relief, try slowing down.
Lily Tomlin

No one answers the phone anymore. They "let the machine get it" to save time. And if you have the time, they'll tell you about all the things they have to do before tomorrow or before dinner or before the kids get home. They have the housework to finish, a deadline at work to beat, children's soccer games to go to, the dry cleaning to pick up, and the exercise class to attend. As one of our friends is fond of saying, we're all as busy as a fiddler's elbow.

Larry Dossey, a physician, coined the term "time sickness" in 1982 to describe the obsessive belief that "time is getting away, that there isn't enough of it, and that you must pedal faster and faster to keep up."[1] By that definition, we're almost all time sick. Who among us isn't busy and in a rush?

Nearly twenty years ago when we were first married and living in Pasadena, we attended the same church as family psychologist and author James Dobson. One Sunday morning, he made a guest appearance in our newlywed class, and in the context of his lesson he said something that got the full attention of every neophyte couple in the room: "Overcommitment and exhaustion are the most insidious and pervasive marriage killers you will ever encounter as a couple." We've never forgotten that. In fact, we've been working at guarding against busyness ever since. Once you realize the potential harm busyness can have on your marriage, you become all the more conscious of how much, or how little, time you spend together each day.

According to a poll by *Marriage Partnership* magazine,[2] here's how much time spouses report spending together each day:

Less than 1 hour: 23%
1–2 hours: 28%
3–4 hours: 26%
More than 4 hours: 22%

It's nearly an equal distribution between less than one hour and more than four. So where do you land on that continuum? If you did the workbook exercise in chapter 1, you already know. But if you didn't, don't even answer for now. Let's be content for the moment to recognize that all of us are busy, and that our busyness is not helping our marriages.

> *The great paradox of our time is that many of us are busy and bored at the same time.*
>
> **Henri Nouwen**

No matter how much time stealing, time stretching, and time bending we attempt, we always find ourselves up against a certain mathematical law: Thirty-two hours' worth of tasks can't be crammed into a twenty-four-hour day. So, we are busy. Nobody's disputing that fact.

The question is, "How busy are you?" We take that back. The real question—the one upon which this chapter hinges—is, "What are you busy doing?"

What Busyness Does to a Marriage

Recent research at the University of Chicago and other places has made it clear that married people, on the whole, are happier, healthier, and wealthier than unmarried people.[3] It's true. Social scientists have been accumulating data for decades, quantifying and measuring exactly what happens to people who become husband and wife, and the news is good. Very good. But researchers also know that when a marriage becomes burdened by busyness, stress fractures eventually appear. What do they look like? Here are a few of the most common ill effects busyness has on marriage.

Busyness Corrupts Your Conversations

We recently received an email from our friend Greg Stielstra, who told us that he and his wife, in managing their household of three children, feel more like air traffic controllers than husband and wife. He said they barely have time to talk because they spend so much time juggling schedules and taxiing kids to and fro. Their conversations consist primarily of sentences like, "Next Tuesday is an early dismissal day for the kids so one of us needs to be home and then take Dominic to soccer practice."

We know the feeling. In fact, most couples do. In a national survey of married couples, researchers found that, on average, we spend less than three minutes of *meaningful* conversation together in a typical day. Yikes! Can you believe it? We are so busy these days that after we coordinate schedules and plan pickups and drop-offs, we don't seem to have enough time to genuinely check in with each other on how we're really doing. Busyness deludes us into thinking that we're conversing when we are actually just trying to make it through the hectic speed of our day.

Busyness Depletes Your Love Life

"Devoting a little of yourself to everything," said Michael LeBoef, "means committing a great deal of yourself to nothing." It's true. When you are scattered too thin, when you're trying to stretch time beyond its limits, you end up with a zero balance in your love bank. The quality of your love life can't help but suffer when you are too busy. In fact, the quality of your love life increases in direct proportion to the amount of time you have to relax. Think about a weekend getaway or even a two-week vacation where your top goal is to decompress and get out of the rat race. What happens to your love life in these times? It inevitably increases, both in quantity and in quality. In fact, physical intimacy takes such a hard hit in a time-starved marriage that later in the book we will devote an entire chapter to purposely seeking out rest and recreation together.

> *Haste manages all things badly.*
>
> **French proverb**

Busyness Steals Your Fun

Busyness is a fun killer. There's no way around it. If you're exhausted from just trying to keep the hamster wheel of life turning, you're never going to enjoy the ride. Think of some of the crazy things you did when you were a dating couple. You were all about fun in those days. Laughter was your third companion on every date. So what happened? You know. Busyness pushed fun out of the commuter car. "Love must rest on trust, honesty, and plain old fun," says author Bill Hybels. "It is only when those foundations are built and maintained that oneness is possible."

Busyness Erodes Your Soul

Perhaps the most corrosive by-product of busyness for a couple is the inevitable erosion of their inner resources. If you are busy enough, long enough, you will become spiritually bankrupt. God will feel absent. Why? Because at the center of every couple's shared lives, underneath the layers of everydayness, an emptiness gradually settles in for even the most committed couples whose spirits have not been nourished. Busyness slowly and steadily wears away spiritual contentment and depletes our relationship of inspiration. Our friend Neil Clark Warren once said, "Whenever inspiration graces your life together, recognize this as one of God's powerful ways of bonding you together so strongly that you can survive every twist of fate for as long as you live." A couple too-long ensconced in the hustle and hurry of one busy week piled upon another will never feel their spirits soar.

How to Battle Busyness and Win

Michigan's Governor Granholm recently issued an official proclamation in her state. "Whereas many Americans are working extremely long hours, taking shorter vacations, and suffering from stress and burnout ... Whereas time pressure, overwork, and over-scheduling have a negative impact on family life, ... therefore be it resolved, that I, Jennifer M. Granholm, Governor of the State of Michigan, do hereby proclaim [this day] as 'Take Back Your Time' Day."[4]

We'd never heard of such a proclamation. It almost made us want to pull up our roots in Seattle and move to the Great Lakes State. Who wouldn't want to live in a place where even the governor is wanting you to not be so busy? If only it were that easy. Unfortunately, it takes more than a proclamation to actually win the war on busyness. Here are a few suggestions for doing just that.

Umm ... Slow Down

Of course, the cure for hurry sickness is to slow down. Lily Tomlin's quote at the beginning of the chapter is one of our favorites:

"For fast-acting relief, try slowing down." If you prefer a more contemplative thinker, here's what Gandhi said: "There is more to life than increasing its speed." Okay. So we all know we should slow down, but how? Well, at the end of reading this sentence, close your eyes, take a deep breath, put your hand over your heart, and feel the beat for about fifteen seconds. Did you do it? If so, you know how something as simple as this can slow you down. But if you didn't, if you kept on reading, let us ask you a question. You seriously don't have time to pause for fifteen seconds before completing this paragraph? If so, we have a more challenging assignment. Try not wearing your watch tomorrow. If you're really brave, take the clock off the wall. Just for a day. You'll be amazed to discover how tuned into time you are and how your watch speeds you up more than you think. It's a little exercise that can't help but make you ease your foot off the gas pedal of your day and slow down.

Examine Your "Secondary Gains"

We have a friend who actually feels complimented when you tell him he looks tired. "Been pushing hard," he'll say with pride. Know someone like this? They view "busy" as a badge of honor. Why? It has to do with something we psychologists call secondary gains. The primary gain of being busy appears to be productivity. But just under the surface, we also gain from running in high gear because it may keep us from reflecting on the deeper issues of our lives—something that tends to scare us. Or perhaps it keeps us from thoughts and feelings, and even people, we dread. Being busy gives us license to arrive late, slip out early, or be absent altogether. And this can apply to the home front as well as work. Busyness can keep us from having a conversation that's long overdue. It can prevent us from confronting an issue that's begging to be addressed. You get the idea. Busyness may be a means of avoiding something the two of you need to discuss. Perhaps it's your mounting financial debt or the lack of a concerted disciplinary approach with your kids. Maybe it's the feeling of drifting apart.

If you're ever going to be successful in wrestling your busyness to the ground, you need to take a serious look at any potential second gains. You need to ask yourself, "What exactly is my busyness getting me besides the belief that I'm getting more done?" Be honest, brutally honest, with yourself as you explore your answer.

Quit Serving Leftovers

Busy people rarely give their best to the ones they love. They serve leftovers. We're not talking about the kind that come from your fridge. We're talking about emotional and relational left-overs — the ones that remain after the prime energy and attention has already been given to others. This

> **Lost time is never found again.**
>
> **Benjamin Franklin**

is sometimes known as sunset fatigue. It's when we are too drained, too tired, or too preoccupied to be fully present with the one we love the most. They get what's left over. And a marriage cannot survive on leftovers forever.

Here's a little trick we learned from our friend John Maxwell. He's one of the most productive men we know, but he makes a conscious effort to give his best time to his wife, Margaret. "Years ago," he told us, "when something exciting happened during the day, I'd share it with colleagues and friends. By the time I got home, I had little enthusiasm for sharing it with Margaret." He went on to say, "I purposely began keeping things to myself until I could share them with her first. That way she never got the leftovers." Of course, this goes for more than just sharing news from our own day. We give our best to our spouse when we give them attention and energy for the things they'd like to talk about as well.

Say No Gracefully

One of the most difficult things some people ever have to do is say no. Yet this little word is one of your strongest weapons in the war against busyness. If you don't believe us, we've got to tell you that we've seen people literally collapse from fatigue, drown in depression, and develop debilitating illnesses because they never said no. Some physicians even call cancer "the disease of nice people."

Surgeon Bernie Siegel tells about one of his cancer patients who never said no. She began to improve, however, after she finally told her boss that she could no longer work extra hours whenever he asked. She began to reclaim her time. Siegel said, "People who neglect their own needs are the ones who are most likely to become ill. For them the main problem often is learning to say no without feeling guilty."[5]

If you suffer from the disease to please, treat it seriously and assert yourself. Begin by making a list of things you have on your plate right now that you'd like to say no to. Discuss them with your spouse or someone else you respect. Chances are he or she can coach you on wielding the mighty power of this little word.

The Business of Eliminating Busyness

We read nearly everything John Ortberg writes. We went to graduate school with John and have long known him to be one of the most down-to-earth writers on heavenly issues you'll ever find. In his book, *The Life You've Always Wanted*, he has a chapter called "An Unhurried Life" in which he tells the story of getting some spiritual direction from a wise friend shortly after moving to Chicago to become the preaching pastor at the megasized Willow Creek Community Church. "I described [to my friend] the pace at which things tend to move in my current setting," John writes. He also told his friend about the fast clip of his family life. "What do I need to do," John asked, "to be spiritually healthy?"

After a quiet moment, his friend finally spoke: "You must ruthlessly eliminate hurry from your life."

Another long pause.

Though I am always in haste, I am never in a hurry; because I never undertake any more work than I can go through with perfect calmness of spirit.

John Wesley

"Okay, I've written that one down," John told him, a little impatiently. "That's a good one. Now, what else is there?" John had a lot to do, and he was talking to his friend long-distance, so, as he puts it, "I was anxious to cram as many units of spiritual wisdom into the least amount of time possible."

Another long pause on the line.

"There is nothing else," his wise friend said. "You must ruthlessly eliminate hurry from your life."[6]

That's it. His spiritual mentor could have given him a laundry list of things to do that would have aligned his spirit with the Almighty. But that's all he suggested. There's nothing else but to eliminate hurry from your life.

We felt compelled to end this chapter with John's story because we fear you might approach our chapter the same way he approached his friend. We fear you'll come to the close of this page and then move on to the next chapter to find out "what else" you can do for your time-starved marriage.

After all, you've read about the negative impact prolonged busyness can have on your marriage and you've read through our suggestions for combating it. That's great. But don't fall into the temptation of thinking that just because you've read this chapter, you will now practice its principles. Don't just "check off" this chapter and then think you're now less busy. You've got to get about the business of ruthlessly eliminating busyness from your relationship.

> *Hurry is not of the devil, it is the devil.*
>
> **Carl Jung**

So take a moment before quickly moving on to part 2 of this book to see "what else" we have to say, and instead take a few minutes to consider how you will put this chapter into practice.

For Reflection

1. What makes you feel most busy? In what areas of your life do you most often feel that you must pedal faster and faster to keep up? Why?

2. Busyness can negatively affect four areas: your conversations, your love life, your ability to have fun, and your spirituality. Which of these four areas is the most negatively affected by your busyness? Why?

3. After reviewing the arsenal of ways to battle busyness in this chapter, what is the one you feel can be most useful to both of you? How and when will you put it into practice?

Workbook Exercise:
Eliminating Hurry from Your Marriage

Both you and your spouse can find this optional workbook exercise in *Your Time-Starved Marriage Workbook* (*for Men/for Women*). Workbooks are available separately at your local bookstore or online at *www.RealRelationships.com*.

Many people who suffer from anxiety disorders will literally change their home environments and what they do outside the home to better manage their anxiety. What if you had to contend with busyness in the same way? What if busyness was a disorder and your well-being hinged on getting it under control? In this workbook exercise you will explore how to do just that.

part 2

getting a grip on
the time of your life

"Do you remember ... the times of your life?"

Eastman Kodak, the film company, turned this question from a 1975 song by Paul Anka into an anthem for their corporation. The tune, when combined with images of heart-tugging snapshots, became the foundation for a highly successful advertising campaign that ran for years. Of course, the song wasn't written for the ad, but it didn't take a marketing wizard to see what it could do for selling film.

And it doesn't take a psychologist to recognize what the same question can do for a marriage. Do you remember the times of *your* life? Whether it's put to music or not, this question evokes a pensive mood that is sure to cause you to reflect on how your life is being lived.

But in this section of the book, part 2, we aren't necessarily all that interested in your doing much thinking about your past, although that certainly has its place. What we want to do in the next four chapters is give you the best tools we know of for grabbing the times of your life—seizing the moments of your marriage—and milking them for all they are worth.

4

time styles: uncovering your unique approach to time

Time management is really a misnomer — the challenge is not to manage time, but to manage ourselves.
Stephen R. Covey

Timex. Bulova. Citizen. Swatch. Casio. Rolex. Fossil. Omega. Seiko. What do you wear?

Almost everyone owns a wristwatch. About half a billion are sold each year. Many of us own more than one. Some collect them by the dozens. Ever since French mathematician and philosopher Blaise Pascal tied a small timepiece to his wrist with a string in the early 1600s, everyone has wanted to wear time on their sleeve.

Today's watches can cost as little as a few bucks to as much as tens of thousands of dollars. They can be functional or fashionable, sometimes both. And more than likely, the one you choose to strap on your wrist says something about you. Think about it. If you knew nothing more about two men than that one wears a classic gold tank watch with a delicate white face and a thin lizard skin strap, and the other wears a black ion-plated Swiss Army number with a sturdy stainless steel bracelet, wouldn't you be able to deduce a bit about their personalities?

You can't deny the fact that our watches say something about who we are. Maybe they even say something about how we approach time itself. Consider the guy who wears a digital watch with a built-in alarm and a minicalculator. Think he approaches time and schedules differently than the man who wears a playful Mickey Mouse wristwatch?

We intend to do much better at sizing up your perspective on time than a cursory look at your wristwatch might reveal. In this chapter you will discover your personal approach to time — something you may have never considered. We call it your "time style."

In addition, by the time you have completed this chapter, you will not only have a better understanding of your own time style but that of your partner as well. And

> *A man with a watch knows what time it is. A man with two watches is never sure.*
>
> **Segal's Law**

this understanding of how your two styles mix and mingle can reveal more than you ever expected. In fact, what you will learn in this chapter may even serve as a defining moment for your relationship. It may help you two crack the code for finding more moments together.

How can we be so confident? Because we've been working on this for years and seen the difference it makes in our own relationship as well as in relationships of those we've taught.

It's tempting to assume that everyone sees time the way we do, but they don't. Each of us comes to time in our own unique way. So we begin with a look at how this happens.

Not All Time Is Created Equal

I'm a night owl. Leslie's an early riser. Some of my most productive time occurs in the wee hours. I wake up sluggish, easing into my morning and gaining full speed about the stroke of noon. Leslie, in contrast, can barely keep her eyes open as the evening grows old. But she's typically up with the sun and amazingly perky as she jumps into a new day. Ironic, isn't it? Seems like this is often the case with couples—one's a night owl and the other's an early riser.

But even if you don't vary in your schedule, you'll likely differ when it comes to either (1) your experience of time in general or (2) your outlook on specific moments in time. Let us explain.

Your time style is basically determined by how you answer two questions:

1. How do I relate to time . . . subjectively or objectively?
2. Which moments in time get most of my attention . . . the present or the future?

Accurately answering these two questions can save you untold hours of "wasted" time in your relationship. They hold the keys to reclaiming the moments you've been missing together.

Subjective versus Objective Timekeeping

How would you answer the following questions?

- When you tell yourself you'll do something at three o'clock, do you mean three o'clock precisely or do you mean three-ish —somewhere around there?
- When you say it's a thirty-minute drive to the store, do you know this because you've timed it or because it just "feels" like thirty minutes to you?
- When you check your schedule for an appointment, do you literally consult a date book or calendar where you continually document your days, or do you just need to think about what else you have going on around that time and "see if it will work"?

If you mean precisely three o'clock, are fairly accurate in your time estimates, and keep a detailed date book, you're probably an *objective* timekeeper. If you are more likely to mean "three-ish," get a "feel" for how long something takes, and you don't carry a Day-Timer or PalmPilot, you're probably a *subjective* timekeeper.

One of these is not better or worse than the other. They just are. Each of us is hardwired differently in our relationship to time. So don't evaluate yourself or your spouse on this continuum. They both have good points and caution flags, but for now we are not concerned with judging the pros and cons of each approach. What we are concerned with is understanding where each of you lands between these two poles. For it is indeed a continuum. Some people are on one extreme or the other, either hard or soft in measuring time, while others are somewhere in between.

In a moment we're going to show how each of you can pinpoint where you land on this continuum. But we need to cover the other continuum before we do that.

Present versus Future Orientation

How would you answer these questions?

- Do you spend more emotional energy enjoying the "here and now" or planning for the "there and then"?
- Are you a goal setter? Do you have a specific place you are headed to years from now, or are you more apt to let the river of life carry you along to your destination?
- Do you spend your money on what you'd like to do today, or are you more likely to give serious consideration to how today's purchase will impact what you can do financially in the future?

If you put more energy into what's around the corner than you do into what's happening right now, if you set specific goals, and if you ponder how a financial decision today will impact what you can do tomorrow, you're likely *future* oriented. If the opposite is true on these questions, you're probably *present* oriented.

On the one hand, some of us hardly give a thought to what's next. The time is now. Right now. We're immersed in what's going on in the present. We don't worry much about the future. That only spoils the present. We'd rather seize the moment. And we can't imagine living life any other way. On the other hand, some of us are perplexed and baffled that anyone could do just that. How do they get anything done, we wonder. How could they not plan for what's about to happen? Why aren't they more strategic about getting where they want to go?

Again, some people are on one extreme or the other, either focused on today or focused on tomorrow, while many are somewhere in between. Before we show you how each of you can zero in on where you land on this continuum, we want to summarize these two dimensions in the diagram below.

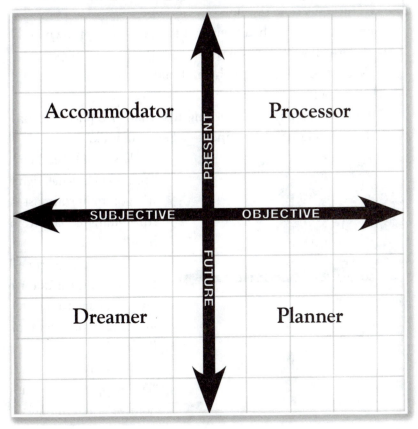

As you can see, the combination of these two dimensions—"subjective versus objective" and "present versus future"—results in four specific time styles. Before you place yourself and your partner into any one of these boxes, let's take a closer look at each one.

The Four Time Styles

The Accommodator

Here you'll find the person who relates to time *subjectively* and is *present* oriented. And because of this, she tries to accommodate time. In other words, she makes room for whatever she wants or whatever she values right now. No matter that her schedule doesn't allow it. She isn't about to let a date book mess up her day. I should know. This is my style (Leslie).

Some time ago we had friends visiting from out of town and I suggested we all walk from our house to a local coffee shop.

"It's just five minutes from here," I said.

"Five minutes?" Les asked.

"Well, maybe ten or something like that," I replied. "I don't know for sure, but it's not far and it's a beautiful walk."

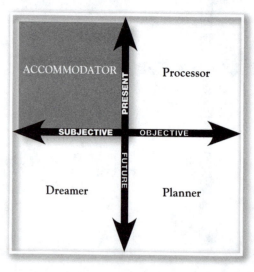

Les shook his head. "You're kidding me, right? It's got to be almost a thirty-minute walk from here."

"I do it all the time," I argued, "and it doesn't seem that far to me. It's just over the Fremont Bridge."

"Exactly," Les said. "I'm happy to do it, but it's not five or ten minutes."

And it wasn't. Like he said, it was about a half hour. But who cares? Well, I guess Les does (he's a Planner). But not me. Like most Accommodators, living in the present and being more subjective than objective, I was happy to accommodate time to take a nice walk and get a bite to eat with our friends.

Accommodators can be punctual, but beware: the quality that allows them to make time for you when you need them can also cause them to run late.

> **The Accommodator says:** "Sure, I have the time."
> **Strengths:** Easygoing, fully present.
> **Challenge:** Setting better boundaries.
> **Under stress becomes:** Disorganized and lacks follow-through.

The Dreamer

This person relates to time *subjectively* but is *future* oriented. He loves what is about to happen and has a vision for it. And like a visitor from the future, he can tell you about the excitement that is just around the bend. No matter that the vision may not be realistic,

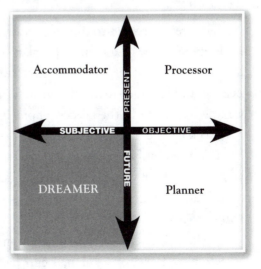

he wants to try it on and simply imagine. He loves what could be.

Our friend Rick fits this style. He had an idea a couple years ago to move his family from Seattle to Europe for a year—"just for the experience." And even though Marvelea is not a "dreamer," she went along with it because she's an Accommodator.

So Rick and Marvelea left their jobs, and along with their two children, trotted around Italy and Switzerland for twelve months. All because Rick had an idea, a dream.

This style doesn't always take on such big proportions. "Sometimes Rick will say something like, 'Let's go to a movie and then listen to jazz tonight,'" Marvelea says. "So I begin to plan my day around this. I think about what I'm going to wear. But when it comes time to go, he could have changed his idea for our evening completely."

"Yeah," Rick chimes in. "If I go online and see that no good movies are playing, I'm on to the next idea. Maybe a barbeque in the backyard, or who knows what."

That's life with a Dreamer, living in the future and fanciful with their time.

The Dreamer says: "I've got a great idea for us."
Strengths: Spontaneous, visionary, optimistic.
Challenge: Becoming more realistic.
Under stress becomes: Immobilized, unreasonable.

The Planner

This person relates to time *objectively* and is *future* oriented. She is all about the schedule and the plan. Like the Dreamer, she has a vision for what could be, but unlike the Dreamer, she's willing to delay gratification to realize it in the future. Planners are prepared. Or at least they're in the process of preparing. They plan their work and work their plan.

I have no problem admitting that I (Les) fall into this style. I'm goal oriented. I'm always thinking about what step to take next. And I can be urgent about what needs to be done now because it will impact what can be done later.

Leslie and I call it the "urgency meter." Because I'm a man of action as I execute a plan, I can become somewhat urgent—

okay, very urgent—about something needing to get done now. It's not because I'm living in the moment, however; it's because I'm planning for the future. I pay a bill the day it arrives so I don't have to worry about it tomorrow. I keep my to-do list short so it won't keep me from taking advantage of a future opportunity. If there's a

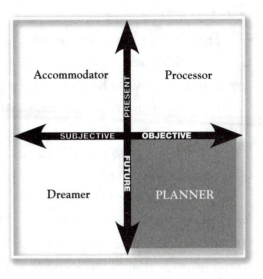

deadline attached to a task, I generally meet it—in advance. Why? Because you never know what good opportunity is just around the corner, and I don't want to miss out on it because I'm not prepared, because I don't have the time or the resources.

If you know what I mean by this internal urgency meter, you're probably a Planner or you live with one. And you probably realize that more than any other time style, Planners are the ones that try to control time. Ask them what time it is and they'll say, "It *should* be one o'clock." This quality generally makes them industrious and productive with their time. They often practice delayed gratification, putting off an immediate pleasure in order to realize a greater payoff later on. So they may not always be punctual, but when they are late, it's usually by their own design.

The Planner says: "I'll be with you in just a minute."
Strengths: Efficient, prepared, takes action.
Challenge: Living more fully in the present (not multitasking).
Under stress becomes: Impatient and insensitive.

The Processor

This person relates to time *objectively* and is *present* oriented. He methodically structures his time and moves at a steady pace. He generally finishes what he starts, and he doesn't start what he can't finish within a reasonable time period. After all, his focus is primarily on the present, not the future.

"Okay, if you go to your File menu and select Print Preview, we can take the next step," Susan says in a composed and soothing voice. "Let me know when you've done that." She works the phones at a computer help desk and she calmly solves one problem after the other. Once she hangs up from one call, she's ready for the next. She'll take a scheduled break and then be back on the phone after lunch. Susan's time style is that of a Processor. She's focused on what she's doing right now. To be content she doesn't require the big picture for the future or a major mission. She simply enjoys the satisfaction of completing her current task.

Some people call this approach to time "Hollywood hours." On the set of a movie, people show up on time. They do what they're supposed

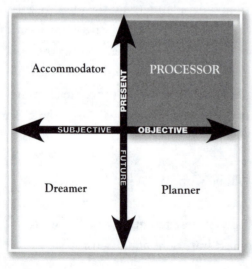

to do in that moment. Only the director and producer worry about the big picture. The other workers aren't focused on the final product that will release months down the line. Members of a movie crew have their specific jobs, and that's what they do. They obey the process. In fact, they have union policies that ensure it. What they don't have is flexibility. You might want the key grip to help hold the boom, or the lighting team to come in a few minutes early to set something up, but they won't. That's not how the process works.

This applies even to lunch. At a certain time, after a certain number of hours, the set shuts down. Lunch is served. After the mandated lunch break, everyone gets back to work, trying to regain the momentum they had in the morning. And you can't make it up by staying late. If you stay even a minute past the cutoff point, everyone gets a significant overtime bonus.

This rigidity doesn't necessarily characterize the Processor, but this approach to time does. The Processor fixes something to a set time and generally sticks to it. He follows the routine. After all, he is objective. If he says he will be there at three o'clock, that's precisely when he will be there—unless something out of his control prohibits it.

> **The Processor says:** "I'll be ready at 9:15."
> **Strengths:** Punctual, disciplined, paced.
> **Challenge:** Relaxing by going with the flow.
> **Under stress becomes:** Compulsive and legalistic.

Taking the Time-Style Marriage Assessment

Before we go much further, you need to realize an important point. Each of us can move in and out of these time styles. We don't land in one box and stay there. A variety of factors—from being hungry, to who we are with—can impact our approach to time in a given moment. Still, there is probably one area in these quadrants where we feel most at home.

You may already know which of these four time styles tends to characterize you best. Or you may feel like you vacillate between two of them. Or maybe you're still scratching your head and wondering which one really describes you best. Whatever the case, we want to help you get a clearer picture of your primary style.

The whole struggle of life is to some extent a struggle about how slowly or how quickly to do each thing.

Sten Nadolny

Not only that, we want to show you how your two styles interact. For example, if you are a Planner married to an Accommodator, there are some predictable predicaments you are going to run into as you contend with your joint schedules. The same is true for a Dreamer married to a Planner or a Processor. Or any of the possible sixteen combinations.

How can we do this for you? By having you take the quick and easy online assessment that we call the Time-Style Marriage Assessment (TSMA). Simply log onto *www.RealRelationships.com*, and you'll find a link for doing just that. And the good news is that it's free. Not only that, there's no way to "fail" this assessment. It simply reveals how you are hardwired in relationship to time. Once both you and your partner know your time styles, turn to the appendix, "Your Personal Time-Style Combinations" on page 137. There you will learn more about the benefits and challenges of the way the two of you approach time. You will also learn how to tap into the best qualities offered by the combination of your two time styles.

So, before you move to the next chapter, take a moment to complete the TSMA. It will take you only ten minutes—and it just may be one of the most important things you ever do to reclaim the moments you've been missing together.

For Reflection

1. Are you more subjective (unscheduled) or objective (scheduled) when it comes to experiencing time and why?

2. Are you more present oriented or future oriented in where you focus your energy? What's your reasoning?
3. Of the four time styles — Accommodator, Dreamer, Planner, or Processor — which one do you most identify with? In which camp do you see your spouse tending to land? How would you describe your combination of time styles (what are its strengths and challenges)?
4. When will you both take the online Time-Style Marriage Assessment (TSMA) and discuss your results? Be specific (we don't want you to miss out on this great tool).

Workbook Exercise:
Are You Fast or Slow?

Both you and your spouse can find this optional workbook exercise in *Your Time-Starved Marriage Workbook (for Men/for Women)*. Workbooks are available separately at your local bookstore or online at *www.RealRelationships.com*.

Since the primary focus of this chapter is the free online Time-Style Marriage Assessment (TSMA), the workbook exercise for this chapter goes a different direction by having you examine another dimension that may be helpful to you. Are you fast or slow? Some couples have a tug-of-war with patience, not giving or getting enough of it. This exercise will help you assess and discuss where you both are on this continuum — "fast," "slow," or somewhere in between.

5

priorities: from finding to making time together

Time is like oxygen — there's a minimum amount that's necessary for survival. And it takes quantity as well as quality to develop a warm and caring relationship.
Armand Nicholi

"If Jim tells me one more time that he can't speak to me because 'the game's on,' I'm going to lose it." Tina's frustration was palpable as she sat next to her uncomfortable husband on the comfortable couch in our counseling office. I (Leslie) glanced quickly at Les to convey the message that this session might get intense. "With satellite TV and all the sports channels we get, a game is always on. Last spring, I thought I'd go crazy with the basketball championships stretching into the summer. Now it's the World Series. Sports have swallowed our relationship."

Tina, thirty-eight, and Jim, forty-one, couldn't stop sparring about Jim's alleged addiction to TV sports. Tina, a former florist, quit her job to stay home when their twin sons were born nearly two years ago. Jim, a graphic designer in a small office he owned with a partner, argued that his wife was overreacting to the situation, and he couldn't understand why she carried on.

"She's crazy. I'm sick of hearing her complaints, especially about the TV," Jim said. "Yes, I love sports. Since when is that a crime? I don't watch as much as I used to and nowhere near what Tina claims."

"Jim keeps all our sets on at the same time," Tina argued, "so that as he moves from room to room, he won't miss anything. And the minute he gets in the car, the radio goes on. Every button is set to a sports station. He always has to know the latest scores. He even falls asleep in bed with the remote in his hand."

"Tina, that's just not true," Jim retorted. He then turned to Les and me as we listened. "Look, I know she's strung out and tired with these little boys—do you think I'm not? That's no reason to explode just because I'm watching a game. Last week, she slammed doors and whined because I had fallen asleep when she wanted to talk. Excuse me, but I don't think I deserved that. I'm a good father—how many men do you know who would take off work for two months after a baby is born? Fortunately, I have an understanding business partner and enough projects in the works for me to be able to do that."

"Do you know what it's like to hear TV sports drone on endlessly, everywhere you go?" Tina asked.

"Not really," Les interjected. "But I know what it's like to hear the two of you drone on about how much you dislike each other."

I cringed as Les said these blunt words. I knew what he was doing, from a therapeutic perspective, but I half expected Jim and Tina to call it quits right on the spot. But they didn't. They did exactly what Les was hoping.

"Wait a second, Doc," Jim said as he looked at Les, "I love Tina."

None of us said a word in that moment. Les slowly moved his gaze from Jim to Tina. Both were quiet.

"I do ... Tina, I really love you," Jim said as he looked at her. He put his hand on her knee and appeared to get choked up. Tina got teary.

Getting Back on Track

It's called a therapeutic turning point—when all the distracting issues clouding a couple's vision, all the meaningless arguments, suddenly fade and they see with clarity what matters most.

That's when I jumped in. "Tina, what's going on for you right now? How do you feel when you hear Jim say that?" I asked.

Tina melted. "He's right," she said through her tears, "I do exaggerate our problems. He's a really great dad ... but I miss him. Where did our time go? Since the twins, we never have time together, and I'm going bonkers."

To make sure nothing punctured this moment of vulnerability, I encouraged Tina to rein in her exaggerated accusations. In the weeks that followed, she took ownership of her tendency to routinely put Jim on the defensive. At the same time, Jim had to stop calling her crazy, since it pushed her hottest of hot buttons. Jim also needed to acknowledge that, to some extent, his behavior was provocative. Les pointed out that his excessive sports watching was an escape, and it was eating up every spare moment of their marriage.

Once Tina moved from demanding to requesting, her diatribes lessened and so did Jim's frustration. In time, Jim agreed to limit his sports watching to the times when Tina wasn't home.

As they started to feel more like a team, they began to discuss ways they could spend more time together. After a few weeks, it was obvious that they were getting back on track. "We've reset our compass," Jim told us. "We're doing a lot better at keeping our eyes on what matters most ... you know, loving each other and making our home the best it can be for these two boys. It's true that keeping our priorities in line, remembering what really matters, seems to create more time for us to be together."

How did they do this? They got practical. Once they determined what mattered most, positive decisions resulted. They decided to join a gym that offers babysitting for toddlers, for example, so that they can work out three times a week together. They both love to be physically active, and this proved to be a wonderful way for them to share time doing something they both enjoyed. They also found a college student, majoring in education, who was looking for a "project" with twins. She now comes in one evening a week, and this provides a Thursday date night for Jim and Tina.

Formal counseling ended after three months, but Jim and Tina continued to make their marriage a priority — and more time together was the result.

Ever feel like Jim and Tina? Ever feel like you've gotten off track and neglected what matters most? Nearly every couple falls into this trap at some point. The reason? In a word, *distractions*. Like Jim, we become distracted by superficial desires and unhealthy obsessions. And like Tina, we lose our cool and get hot and bothered by our own irrational exaggerations. In short, we get out of balance. Our relationship gets absorbed by second-tier "priorities" that eat up our time and keep us from moving toward our goal.

If you are feeling off track, this chapter will help you realign the wheels of your relationship and balance your relational tires. It will get you back on the road you were meant to travel, eliminate distractions, and keep you from veering off your course.

How to Make Time

One of the most common fallacies of time is that you can "find" it. Turn to nearly any business journal or women's magazine and you'll read about ways to "find more time." We talk about time as if it is hidden under the cushion of a chair in our living room or stuck behind a piece of furniture in the basement. Truth is, we'll never find more time. But we can "make" more time.

Time is made whenever we decide what matters most. A top priority gets more time. If you decide that collecting stamps is the most important thing in your life, you will begin to schedule your day around it, you will spend your money on it, and you will talk about it. Because you prioritize it, you'll make decisions that create more time for it.

"The reason most goals are not achieved is that we spend our time doing second things first," said business author Robert J. McKain. And he's exactly right. We may say that our marriage comes first, but

> *You will never find time for anything. If you want time you must make it.*
>
> **Charles Buxton**

that doesn't matter if we devote our time to what's lower on our list. Saying it's a priority and making it a priority are two different things. So if you are merely giving lip service, and not your time, to making your marriage a priority, here are some practical ways of getting back on course and making more time for your marriage.

Do the Right Thing

Consider what's right for your relationship. What are the activities you know are bound to bring you together as a couple? For the two of us, it's having a date night. We know our marriage suffers when we don't make time for this each week. And it can be a struggle. Our travel schedule interferes. Babysitters are not always available when we need them. It's expensive. It's tough to leave our two boys at home. We have lots of reasons to neglect our date night, but we know it's the right thing to do.

By the way, just because you know what's right to do doesn't mean you have to do it perfectly. Don't set yourself up to give up on something good just because you can't always do it well. "Concentrate first on doing the right things, then on doing things right," said renowned management expert Peter Drucker. "There is nothing so wasteful as doing the wrong things well." Sometimes just getting out the door together for a couple hours is all we can manage.

> *You cannot protect your priorities unless you learn to decline, tactfully but firmly, every request that does not contribute to the achievement of your goals.*
>
> **Ed Bliss**

No dinner reservation, no plan. That's okay. It's the right thing to do even when we don't do it exactly right.

Know What to Leave Undone

Tharon and Barbara Daniels are two of the most easygoing people we know. They work hard and are often busy, but as we've observed their marriage for more than a decade, we've noticed that they always seem to make time for each other. These days they have an empty nest, and that makes it easier, but when we first met them they had two teenagers at home.

"Some years ago when we were moving fast with two active kids, I made a decision to give up golf," Tharon told us. "It sounds silly, but golf was eating up my entire day off. Golf was taking valuable time away from being with Barbara, and she's more important to me than golf." These days Tharon plays plenty of golf, but for a season of his life, he knew it was best to leave it alone. His sacrifice made more time for what mattered most.

His decision isn't for everyone—some spouses are actually easier to live with when they have an individual activity they enjoy. The point is that if you want to make more time to spend together, you can probably find something to leave undone. This means saying no, tactfully but firmly, to those things that can so easily rob us of our time together. We'll have more to say on this in chapter 7. For now, you may want to whisper the prayer

> *Besides the noble art of getting things done, there is the noble art of leaving things undone. The wisdom of life consists in the elimination of nonessentials.*
>
> **Lin Yutang**

of Elizabeth Fry, an English Quaker from the eighteenth century: "O Lord, may I be directed what to do and what to leave undone."

Make an "If I Do Nothing Else Today" List

What's on your "to-do" list today? The Pilates session? The hamper spilling with laundry? The four calls you meant to make yesterday? Getting the oil in your car changed? Let's face it, the list of to-dos for most of us is endless. And yet we browbeat ourselves with guilt over never completing the list when it would probably remain undone even if we had a clone.

So here's the deal. If your list is as long as a New York phone book, accept it. You've got a lot to do, and you're never going to get to all of it. So place a priority on what you want to have accomplished by the time your head hits the pillow at night. What matters most today in the time you have with your spouse? This is not some fancy-pants approach to outsmarting the clock. Simply write this phrase, then complete it:

If I do nothing else *today* for my marriage, I will …

Stumped for ideas? Here are some examples: "If I do nothing else today for my marriage, I will take a twenty-minute walk with my spouse around the neighborhood ... I will surprise my partner with a relaxing meal at a restaurant ... I will pray for my spouse to feel less stressed." You get the idea. Each day you can think about the one thing you will do to *make* more time together. Once that thing becomes a priority, you'll give it the time it requires.

Make a Margin for the Unexpected

Henry Kissinger, the secretary of state of the United States in the mid-1970s, is known for his expertise in the complex and delicate world of foreign policy. But he's also known for saying, tongue in cheek, "There cannot be a crisis next week; my schedule is already full."

A good life, like a good book, should have a good margin. The most winsome people in the world are the people who make you feel that they are never in a hurry.

F. W. Boreham

We have a feeling you know just what he means. When you're booked wall-to-wall with one activity after the other, you don't have room for the unexpected. And if there's one thing you can always expect, it's the unexpected. Whether it's a traffic jam that slows you down, a miscalculation that delays a project, or a misunderstanding that throws you off, the unexpected is inevitable. So make a margin for it. Allow some extra time that will keep you from feeling frazzled.

We call it a cushion in our relationship. To be honest, we run our clocks by it. If we need to get up at 7:00 a.m., we make a point of getting up at 6:50 a.m. This bit of sneaky self-deception provides us with a bit of cushion. It may not work for you, but you can find other ways to make time by making margins in your day. Whether it's leaving the office ten minutes earlier, buying Christmas presents months in advance, or scheduling the babysitter to arrive earlier than you actually need her, margins reduce the mayhem and make a little more time for your marriage.

Purge Your Schedule of Distractions

The ferry people. That's how they're known in our city of Seattle. They live on Bainbridge Island or Vashon, and if they are in downtown Seattle, the only way home is by ferry. It's a short ride but the only ride. Consequently, their lives depend upon the ferry schedule. If they are out to eat and the last ferry for the night is about to launch, you'll see a fair percentage of the restaurant nearly stand up in unison to make their boat. They could be in the middle of an amazing story or still be nibbling on their delectable dessert, but nothing will keep them from staying on schedule.

It begs the question: if we can become slaves to a ferry schedule, letting nothing distract us from catching the vessel before it departs, can't we give the same kind of priority to our marriage? Can't we keep distractions from intruding upon the time we prioritize for our relationship? Of course.

> *When people complain that they don't have enough time to do something, what they're really saying is that the thing is not a priority, and what they are doing is choosing another activity in its place.*
>
> **Allison Carter**

That's the bottom line of this chapter — to purge our schedules of whatever we can so that we are always conscious of what matters most. Pulitzer prize–winning playwright and screenwriter, Sidney Howard, said it nicely: "One half of knowing what you want is knowing what you must give up before you get it."

So what can you give up to make more time for your marriage? In the next chapter we're going to help you answer this question more definitively by showing you how to prioritize your "prime time" together.

For Reflection

1. A major step toward "making more time" is to put first things first and do what matters most. Why can it be so difficult to set your priorities and allow them to direct your decisions?
2. Identify a specific time when you felt like your priorities got out of whack—when you were distracted—and as a result you ended up wasting or misusing your time. Looking back, what caused the distraction and, more importantly, what can you do to safeguard yourself from having this happen again?
3. What's one thing that you could leave "undone" for a while? Something that would give you more time together and would be okay if it was not accomplished?

Workbook Exercise:
How to Make More Quality Time

Both you and your spouse can find this optional workbook exercise in *Your Time-Starved Marriage Workbook (for Men/for Women)*. Workbooks are available separately at your local bookstore or online at *www.RealRelationships.com*.

Most of us would agree that the amount of time a couple has together is vitally important. And most of us would quickly follow that up by saying that the amount of time matters very little if much of that time isn't also quality time. Well, this workbook exercise will help you delve into identifying exactly what each of you means by "quality time." Not everyone agrees on what it means to put first things first. Do this exercise and you'll discover why.

6

prime time:
maximizing the minutes
that matter most

We live in a moment of history where change is so speeded up that
we begin to see the present only when it is already disappearing.
R. D. Laing

"You've got to be kidding, right?" His question was laced with sarcasm.

"Gee, that's an interesting idea." Her tone and the look on her face made her frustration hard to miss.

We'd asked the simple question that we ask nearly every couple who comes to us for help: *When was the last time you had a date night for just the two of you?*

We could take up the rest of this chapter just listing all the reasons this couple gave us for not spending time together. Three kids, their schools, sports teams, lessons, recitals, elderly parents who need care, household chores, car maintenance, home repairs and remodeling, and church attendance with a slew of activities. Oh, and then there were their two jobs. And occasional overtime.

By the time the week or month or year had raced by for this couple, there wasn't a spare inch of time for them to spend a quality evening together.

So we asked the question again: "When was the last time you had a date night for just the two of you?" And we got the predictable response. They looked at each other, sighed, and said, "It's been a long time."

That isn't the way it's supposed to be. Most couples—maybe all couples—go into marriage determined to spend time together, just the two of them, just like before they were married. But somewhere down the line, shortly after the first baby enters the picture or maybe after a big job promotion, life gets more complicated, more demanding, more jam-packed.

But even before the first baby arrives, when a couple is seemingly footloose and fancy-free, busyness can consume them, and the moments and minutes that define a marriage as romantic and loving gradually slip away. Marriage, in other words, begins to take a backseat to our schedules.

In this chapter we aim to help you change that. We're not going to harp on having a date night, as important as that can be. Instead, we want to reintroduce you to some spare minutes—some defining moments—you're probably leaving on the table. In other words, we want to show you some spare time that you probably don't even know you have.

Defining a "Defining Moment"

A curious thing happens as the pace of our lives grows faster and faster—our definition of a "moment" grows shorter and shorter, moving our awareness of time into ever tinier increments. By cramming each day so full of activities and events, we leave ourselves no time to actually experience them in any meaningful way. By the time we're into our current event we're already thinking about our next one. Consequently, our meaningful moments last about as long as an ice cube in a frying pan. They disappear so quickly we don't even know what we missed.

So let's start by exploring exactly what is meant by "a moment." Webster defines it as "a point of time." Okay. That's a little too brief for our purposes. But a little more light can be shed by unpacking this word's Latin origin. *Moment* comes from *movimentum*, where we get our word *momentum*, and it literally means "to turn the scales." In other words, a moment makes a difference. It moves us.

Psychologically, a moment is the occasion when your mind is most apt to absorb the full effect of an event—no matter how small. It's what is meant by a "defining moment." In other words, if your mind is prepared, a brief point of time can change you. It can move you. It can tip the scales toward love.

> *Most men pursue pleasure with such breathless haste that they hurry past it.*
>
> **Søren Kierkegaard**

Remember in chapter 2 when we said that your marriage is defined by how you spend your time? This is what we were getting at. Marriage is a series of moments, little points in time that accumulate one after the other, every day. And each of these moments, if maximized, can tip the scales of love. Marriage is not about waiting for the big events. When we spend our lives looking for the next big thing, we rush right past the "in-between" moments of marriage. Think about it. The reality is that these interims actually make up the biggest portion of our lives. If we treat them as insignificant, that's exactly what they become. But they can offer so much more. If we set our mind to be present in them and experience them fully, they promise to fill our marriage with life and love.

Tipping the scales toward love depends on being "mindful" of your moments.

How to Milk the Moment

"Get Jackson to look this direction; his face is in the shade," I said to Leslie.

"He wants to feed the ducks."

"I know, but if you want me to take this picture so we can get to Train Town you've got to get him to look over here," I said impatiently as our two-year-old was tossing a few bread crumbs into the water while I teetered uncomfortably on the edge of the dock to try and capture the shot.

You will find as you look back upon your life that the moments when you have truly lived are the moments when you have done things in the spirit of love.

Henry Drummond

"I know—oh, that duck is really aggressive," Leslie laughed. So did Jack.

"You're not listening to me. There might be a long line at the train." I was feeling exasperated as I tried to get the light just right and quickly compose a photo that would capture the moment.

"I am listening," Leslie said, "but you seem more concerned with the schedule than you do with this moment. Jack is really having fun here. Who cares if we miss the train?"

She was right. Here we were at Stanley Park in Vancouver, British Columbia, on a sunny Saturday afternoon. We had no agenda except to have a good time, and I got it into my head that the best way to do this was to ride the little train with our toddler. So I was directing a self-imposed schedule that removed me from the moment. I was missing the fun right in front of me. Feeding ducks. Laughing. These are the points in time that life and love are made of. And I was rushing right past them.

Ever done that? Ever missed out because your mind was somewhere else? Silly question, we know. Who hasn't done this? Rushing is the surest way to miss the meaning of a moment. Conversely, the greatest guarantee for milking a moment for all it's worth is to wrap your mind around it completely. A sense of "mindfulness" is the key to maximizing your moments.

Mindfulness is a way of being that puts you fully in the here and now without the pressure or anxiety of staying on schedule. All your senses are awake and heightened, and you are fully comfortable in the present. When you are mindful, you are momentarily rooted with nowhere to go and no need to rush. You aren't bored or anxious. Instead, you are fully present.

Needless to say, mindfulness is one of the greatest gifts you will ever give to yourself or your spouse. "The most precious gift we can offer others is our presence," said Thich Nhat Hanh. "When mindfulness embraces those we love, they will bloom like flowers."

A Few "Mundane" Moments Worth Mentioning

Now that we've defined "a moment" and explored how to milk it, allow us to note a few of the most overlooked moments in marriage. Chances are that you already take advantage of some of them. You use them to tip the scales toward love. But you may not always use them to full advantage.

1. Making a Moment: When You Say Hello

Fido may do a better job than you do of greeting your spouse when he or she comes home at the end of the day. If you have a family dog, you know what it means to be loyal, enthusiastic, and totally focused on the greeting ritual. But even if you don't, you can still learn a lesson from "man's best friend." How you greet each other sets the tone for the time that follows. If your opening words to your spouse are about having left the garage door open or remembering to pay a bill, you're missing out on a great moment. A loving greeting, a tender touch, a kiss, or an embrace are sure to tip the scales in the right direction. The key to doing this, as with all meaningful moments, is to prepare your mind for it. As you're walking up your front steps, think through how you'd like to say hello and establish a connection.

2. Making a Moment: When You Say Good-Bye

Just as how we say hello offers the possibility of a positive moment, so does a good good-bye. Perhaps the most famous and loving of all good-byes was the one William Shakespeare created between Romeo and Juliet:

> Good night, good night! Parting is such sweet sorrow,
> That I shall say good night till it be morrow.

Now *that's* a good-bye. We're not saying every good-bye is going to be this dramatic — at least we hope not. But it does underscore the value of how we say farewell. Whether it be in the morning before work or before an out-of-town trip separates you for longer, a good good-bye is another moment to tip the scales of time toward love. The key here is simply to be mindful of the good-bye. If you say, "I'll miss you," mean it. Allow your eyes to linger on your spouse for that moment. Leave him or her with a loving wink, if that comes naturally. But most of all, be mindfully present.

3. Making a Moment: When You Go to Sleep

Some of the most important minutes of your marriage can be the ones you spend together just before you fall asleep. But far too many couples waste this opportunity. They don't give it a second thought. They doze off to late-night chatter on the television, a book that makes them drowsy, or maybe the sound of a machine that blocks out distractions. Of course, there's nothing wrong with any of these things, but couples miss out on one of their best opportunities to make a meaningful connection. They end their day stuck in a rut of simply falling asleep in the same bed, when by connecting, they could be dozing off to much sweeter dreams.

If you're like us, you don't always go to bed at the same time — one of you is a night owl and the other an early riser. But this doesn't mean you have to sacrifice pillow talk. Just take a few minutes before the first one of you dozes off. Lie beside each other and talk or pray. Even if one of you stays awake into the wee hours, you'll at least have experienced that prime time of connection.

4. Making a Moment: When You Have a Tough Day

We all have low periods — times when we are not at our best. And again, these are moments ripe with potential to tip the scales. To do so, it may help to know what recent research has discovered about the genders. After a tough day, women are more likely than men to criticize their spouses, while men tend to respond to daytime stress by withdrawing from their mates.[1] Whatever the gender dispositions dictate, don't allow a tough day to come between you and your spouse. As your partner clams up or gets snippy, as the case may be, tip the scales in your favor by being mindful of the tough circumstances. Give your partner some grace, and you'll recoup countless minutes that might otherwise be spent sulking. How can you do this? By letting her know you understand that her day didn't go the way she wanted. By being accepting of a temporary bad mood, rather than trying to get him to instantly change or denying that he feels bad altogether. You can offer your spouse grace by loving him or her anyway.

5. Making a Moment: When You're in a Routine

Believe it or not, most of the important moments in a marriage occur out of habit. These habits are known as "rituals." Marriage and family therapist William Doherty defines marital rituals as "social interactions that are repeated, coordinated, and have positive emotional significance."[2] Basically, this is a routine time to mindfully reconnect as a couple. It's a scheduled moment, mutually decided on, that cuts a new groove in your day or week. A common example is a cup of coffee after dinner. "You tell the kids to go play and leave you alone," says Doherty. "That is the clear sign that you are making the transition to couples time." Then you talk about personal stuff, like how you are feeling or what's weighing on your mind. There is no logistics talk about the kids' next soccer games. There is no problem-solving for the family. And you keep any conflict out of the conversation.

Keep in mind that one person's ritual might be another's boring routine. Every couple is different. Les and I run errands together on Saturday morning. It would be more efficient if he or I did the errands separately, but that is not the point. Marital rituals are not about being efficient; they are about connecting.

6. Making a Moment Last

Memories compound when they are experienced with someone you love. That's why we want to leave you in this chapter with one final thought about maximizing your moments. If you really want to get the most out of them, you'll learn to turn them into a memory.

Most people don't lead their life; they accept their life. They wait for memorable experiences to happen, never giving a thought to creating an experience that will make a memory. However, some of the best memories you will ever have can come from making them happen—even on an otherwise mundane day.

"Remember when we went to the top of Smith Tower?" Leslie asked me just the other day. "I'm so glad we did that."

I am too. We were downtown in Seattle getting a driver's license renewed at the Department of Motor Vehicles—about as mundane as you can get—when we decided on a whim to duck into the old forty-two-story Smith Tower and ride the elevator to the top. Smith Tower was the tallest building in Seattle until 1969, but it's now dwarfed by the seventy-three-story Columbia Tower and other high-rises. But on this day we felt like we were on top of the world, just the two of us, as we stole a few

> *We do not know the true value of our moments until they have undergone the test of memory.*
>
> **Georges Duhamel**

moments while doing errands. Talking together in the "Chinese Room" on the top floor as we looked down on the Mariner's Stadium and took in the view of Mount Rainier and Puget Sound didn't just happen. We made it happen. And now it's a memory we're reliving more than three years later.

Memories don't find us; we find them. We *make* memories. Lewis Carroll said, "It's a poor sort of memory that only works backward." We've got to be on the lookout for them.

For Reflection

1. Recall an experience together from a year ago or so that you still hold as a meaningful moment. What made it so and why, specifically, is it still in your memory bank?

2. Each moment of our married lives provides an opportunity to tip the scales toward love. When was the last time you remember doing this, when you were mindful of moving your relationship toward love? Be specific.

3. When you consider otherwise mundane moments in your marriage, which one of these times holds the most promise for you and your spouse to connect: saying hello, saying good-bye,

having pillow talk before you fall asleep, or when one of you is having a tough day?

4. What marital routine or ritual helps you to connect? If you can't think of one, brainstorm with your spouse on how to create such a ritual.

Workbook Exercise:
Making Your Mundane Moments Count

Both you and your spouse can find this optional workbook exercise in *Your Time-Starved Marriage Workbook (for Men/for Women)*. Workbooks are available separately at your local bookstore or online at *www.RealRelationships.com*.

If you're looking for a practical way to prepare your mind for moments in your marriage that might otherwise slip through your hands, look no further. This workbook exercise provides a proven tool for becoming more mindful of common moments and shows you how to maximize the ones in your relationship that will mean the most.

---

part 2: getting a grip on the time of your life

7

time bandits: catching your time stealers red-handed

Time sneaks up on you like a windshield on a bug.
Jon Lithgow

A man walked into a Burger King in Ypsilanti, Michigan, at 7:50 a.m., flashed a gun, and demanded cash. The clerk said he couldn't open the cash register without a food order. When the wannabe robber ordered onion rings, the clerk said they weren't available for breakfast. The frustrated man stormed out of the restaurant.

Another man walked into a convenience store in St. Louis, put a twenty-dollar bill on the counter, and asked for change. When the clerk opened the drawer, the man pulled a gun and asked for all the cash in the register. The man took the cash from the clerk and fled, leaving his twenty-dollar bill on the counter. So how much did he get from the drawer? Fifteen bucks.

In Missouri, a guy trying to pawn a stolen bracelet was apprehended by police when the pawn shop owner recognized the jewelry — it was his wife's.

In West Virginia, a knife-wielding mugger accepted a three-hundred-dollar check from his victim. The thief was arrested the next day while trying to cash the check.

In Tennessee, a burglar realized he'd left his Nikes at the home he'd just robbed. So he returned and asked the lady of the house if she'd seen his shoes. She called the cops, and the guy was arrested.

The mistakes criminals make could fill a book. In fact, they have. Leland Gregory's *The Stupid Crook Book* reveals dozens of real-life stories about captured criminals who are so dumb you almost feel sorry for them.

The stories are hard to resist. After all, who doesn't like to hear about a foiled bandit who gets caught red-handed? That's exactly what this chapter is dedicated to. Here we want to show you how to catch the most common time bandits of your day. But beware. These crooks are far smarter than the inept criminals you just read about. These time stealers are so subtle you may not even be aware of how much time they are stealing from your marriage.

Of course, there are literally dozens of time bandits walking off with time you could have spent on each other, but the following four are the most common and the most sneaky.

Unfinished Business

Far and away, one of the greatest time bandits prowling around your relationship is the past. Your present is inextricably linked to your past. I (Les) wrote an entire book about it called *Shoulda Coulda Woulda*, so I can assure you that I've given this topic some serious study. Your past can be very crafty when it comes to robbing you of your present. Make no mistake, when you are weighed down by regret, pain, or guilt over things that happened two decades ago or two hours ago, you will no longer be able to live fully in the present. As long as you are gazing over your shoulder, you will feel unfinished.

Unfinished business takes on a life of its own and consumes your time like few competitors. Why? Because the brain remembers incomplete tasks or failure longer than any success or completed activity. Researchers call it the "Zeigarnik effect."[1] Once a project is complete, the brain no longer gives it priority or active working status. But regrets have no closure. The brain continues to spin the memory, trying to come up with ways to fix the mess and move it from active to inactive status. But it can't—not until you work to close it.

If you need to gain closure on anything from your past, the first place to begin is where it hurts. Healing your hurts, particularly if they run deep, is essential to feeding your time-starved marriage, not to mention your own emotional health. Why? Because healing the pain from your past (being hurt in a previous relationship, for example) protects you from repeating the pain in your present marriage. This may sound strange, but if we never come to terms with our past pain, we use our marriage as a means to make it right. The trouble is, marriage was never designed to do that. You'll just continue to repeat relationship problems and replay your pain again and again. That's why the past can be such a gigantic time stealer.

> The only use of a knowledge of the past is to equip us for the present. The present contains all that there is. It is holy ground.
>
> Alfred North Whitehead

Regret about your past, at best, distracts you. At worst, it devastates you. "Look not mournfully into the past, it comes not back again," said poet Henry Wadsworth Longfellow. "Wisely improve the present, it is thine." And it is. The present is what we own. It is holy ground whenever the past is not contaminating it.

So if you are carrying unfinished business from your past, don't allow it to steal another moment from your present. Do the work you need to find closure and move forward. What will this mean for you? Once you identify the loose ends of pain from your past, you'll need to work on resolving them. You may need to apologize to someone you've hurt or forgive someone who's hurt you. You may need to return something that's not yours or regain something that rightfully belongs to you. The possibilities are endless. But don't deny the fact that you may also need a few sessions with a trusted counselor who can provide professional guidance for your situation. The goal is to deal with the unfinished business from your past by doing whatever you can to close it. And be assured that whatever path is required for you to gain this closure, you'll be amazed by how much time you reclaim for your marriage by doing so.

Technology

Some guys are car freaks. Some are sports nuts. Some are golfers. Me? I'm a gadget guy. I love the latest technology. Call me a nerd if you like, I can't help it. Whether it be my cell phone, my laptop, or my television, I love the latest and greatest. And some time ago, when I first heard of something called wi-fi, I was giddy. A wireless network in my own home! No more wires! I couldn't believe it. I could use a computer anywhere in my abode and not be tethered to the wall. Maybe it's the fact that we live just four or five miles from the most technologically tricked-out house on the planet, owned by Bill Gates himself, but I thought wi-fi was beyond cool.

Now Leslie and I could work, pay bills, or check our email from just about any corner of the house: kitchen, living room, patio, even the bedroom. And since we have two small children, a mortgage, and the same twenty-four hour days as everyone else, the wireless network was just what I needed to carve out more quality time for Leslie and me and our family. Or so I thought.

On the first day of my new wireless life, I checked the headlines of a half dozen newspapers while sitting at the breakfast table.

I scanned the television listings for my evening's viewing. And I checked my course enrollments for my upcoming college class. I was hooked. Instant information wherever I wanted it! That night, after tucking our boys in, we were in bed—just me, Leslie, and my Sony laptop. I needed one more fix, a peek at the bank balance and a look at my email. Leslie, on the other hand, needed to talk.

"When you're done with that, I want to tell you about my day tomorrow," she said.

"Okay, go ahead," I said as I clicked away on my keyboard.

"Can we talk without that thing in our bed?" she said, pointing at my computer.

Uh-oh. This isn't good, I thought. Thankfully, I screened out my first impulsive response: *Why don't you instant message me?*

"Of course," I said out loud as I quickly powered down.

In less than twenty-four hours it had become painfully obvious: the wireless network that was making it so much easier for me to be online was also making it harder for me to pay attention to Leslie.

Who'd have thought that with all the technology designed to give us more time—the microwave ovens, cell phones, email, the Internet, TiVo, iPods, PalmPilots, BlackBerrys—we'd be cramming all those "extra moments" we've saved with even more time-consuming technological wizardry? The trouble is that, with all the gizmos and gadgets, we feel more frenzied, more harried, more out of breath than ever before. Seems ironic, but the very things we think are going to save us time often end up stealing it.

> *I find television very educating. Every time somebody turns on the set, I go into the other room and read a book.*
>
> **Groucho Marx**

Do we still have wi-fi? Yes. But I now control it more than it controls me—and it never enters the bedroom. My TiVo? Still working on that one, but I'm getting better. Seriously, if we aren't careful, technology can delude us into thinking we're saving time for our marriage when just the opposite is happening.

Impatience

Unhappy fans voiced their displeasure when Scott Hoch refused to hit his nine-foot birdie putt on the second play-off hole of the 2003 Ford Championship at Doral in Miami, Florida. As darkness fell, Hoch was unsure about the lay of the green. So the tournament's sudden-death finish was delayed until the next morning, when many fans could not attend.

Hoch sank his putt the next morning and then birdied a third play-off hole to win nine hundred-thousand dollars. Had Hoch tried to finish the tournament on Sunday, he probably would have lost. In the dwindling light, Hoch, who has had five eye operations, thought the putt would move left. His caddie saw it the other direction. The morning light proved the caddie right.[2]

How about you? Do you have the kind of patience Scott Hoch does? Not if you're like most people. Most of us want what we want now. We can't wait. So we overextend our budget, our credit, and our calendars. We toss delayed gratification on its ear and make a beeline toward whatever we impulsively want. If this damage on our pocketbooks wasn't bad enough, this same impatience infects our relationships, especially our marriages. We become short with each other. We expect our spouse to do what we want when we want. We hurry our spouse to finish a sentence, to get to the bottom line. We grow weary of waiting, even for a moment, if he or she is a bit late. Impatience steals intimacy from our relationship by infusing it with intolerance, irritation, and annoyance.

"Serenity now!" If you were a fan of the 1990s television phenomenon called *Seinfeld*, you immediately recognize that phrase.

The episode featured a subplot about Frank, the father of main character George. Whenever Frank feels tense, he is to lower his blood pressure by calmly saying, "Serenity now." Frank, unfortunately, doesn't get the idea that this phrase is to be said slowly with a deep breath for a soothing effect. Instead, whenever he is frustrated,

> *Our patience will achieve more than our force.*
>
> **Edmund Burke**

he shouts out the phrase in anger. Like a lot of us, he's demanding to have "serenity now!" No time to cultivate it. No time to wait.

Don't allow yourself to get caught in the same comical trap. Impatience corrodes your time like few other poisons, eating away at what could otherwise be a pleasant moment.

It's tempting to justify impatience by telling ourselves, "This is just how I act when I'm in a hurry. The real me, though, is more loving, and my spouse knows that." Are you sure? Take a good look at this "temporary" trait and be sure it isn't becoming a permanent resident. Giving impatience the boot may be one of the most important things you can do to reclaim the time you've been missing from your marriage.

The Clock

Okay, okay. We can almost hear you as we're writing these words. "What?" you ask. "How does the clock steal our time?" That's a fair question. We have nothing against clocks. In fact, we have a huge clock in our home that nearly every guest comments on. And when it's time to change the clocks in our home around daylight savings time, it becomes painfully obvious how many clocks we own. So relax. We're not fanatical here. In fact, we only want to tell you a story.

It's an old tale of a village that bought a fancy clock tower. Sometime after it was installed, a visitor to the town discovered that all the people were sleeping during the day and working at night. When he questioned them about this, they answered, "We have the most unique town in America. After we got our new clock, we began to notice that the sun kept rising earlier and earlier every morning. Finally the day-time hours were dark and the night hours were light. We are petition-ing the president for special recog-nition as the only town in America with such a situation."

> *I must govern the clock,*
> *not be governed by it.*
>
> **Golda Meir**

As it turned out, of course, the new clock had been running slower and slower, all because sparrows were roosting inside it. The point? The people of the village were so enamored by their clock that they allowed it to control them instead of the other way around.

And that's the potential problem with clocks. If we aren't care-ful, they can make us their slaves. How? Well, consider how many times you say something like: "Hurry up, or we'll be late! You've only got five minutes!" The clock can turn our lives into a race. It's nearly inevitable. You can't extinguish our reliance on time pieces. We'd have chaos. But if we surrender completely to the clock, it spins our relationships out of control as well.

The point is simple. Don't always give in to the tyranny of the clock. Linger over a latte together every once in a while, even if you're running late. If you have a deadline to meet, don't be irre-sponsible, but don't be a time tyrant either. It's a fine line to walk. It requires balance — something those driven solely by the clock seldom have.

Overactivity

Okay, so we said there were four sneaking time bandits we wanted to highlight. And we have done just that. But we want to squeeze one more onto the list. It's so important. We've just got to add one more.

Ever used that strategy on your own list?

We're only doing so here to illustrate a point. We're pushing one more thing onto the agenda after we did what we agreed to. Doing so is exactly what this brazen time bandit requires. Once the slate is full and the dates are booked, this one comes rumbling in and bullies its way onto the already filled schedule. Especially if you have kids. So if you're a parent, take note.

Overactivity, the close cousin of overcommitment, is not so sneaky at all. It's the most obvious time bandit around. You recognize it the moment it appears in your home, trying to show up on your calendar. "We've just got to make this work," we say as we hurriedly make new arrangements and move things around in our date book, as if it were an unexpected guest looking for a place to sleep. But overactivity has no intention of resting. It can take your time for all it's worth and never once blink in the process. In fact, it's the only time bandit that we announce upon its arrival. "Look at this schedule!" we say in amazement. "Can you believe all we've got to do?"

So rather than expound on the obvious, namely that overactivity will steal your time, allow us to make a fundamental point that may be just what you need to hear to keep this one from robbing you blind. If your family car has become a taxicab for running kids to church activities, school events, and children's sporting events, realize that you don't have to do it all. You don't. Nowhere is it written that to be a good parent you have to sign your children up for everything and spend all your "free" time shuttling them around and attending each and every event.

Give overactivity a kick in the seat of the pants by closely examining what you might drop from your long list. You might hold a family meeting to talk about what regaining this time as a family would mean to all of you. Then again, don't feel guilty about trimming the activity list using your own good judgment.

Stealing Your Time Back

Each of the time bandits we've noted in this chapter has nothing to do with external circumstances and everything to do with your choices. So, before we leave this chapter, we want to underscore the fact that you, and you alone, are the gatekeeper to these time stealers. Whether it be allowing your past to contaminate your present, the seductive lie that all technology saves you time, the weakness of impatience, slavery to the clock, or overactivity, none of these will steal your time unless you decide to do nothing about them. In other words, ultimate protection from these time robbers comes from the choices you make to guard yourself against them.

In *Choices*, Frederick F. Flach writes, "Most people can look back over the years and identify a time and a place at which their lives changed significantly. Whether by accident or design, there are moments when, because of readiness within us and collaboration with events occurring around us, we are forced to seriously reappraise ourselves and the conditions under which we live and to make certain choices that will affect the rest of our lives."[3]

So as we conclude this chapter and part 2 of this book, we want to leave you with a challenge. Reappraise your life and the conditions under which the two of you live. What choices can you make to steal back the time your marriage has been robbed of? The exercise on the next page will help you do just that.

Oh, but one more story of an inept crook: A woman was working one night in a Honey Baked Ham store. The store was equipped with security cameras, and she was watching the small, black-and-white monitors when she saw a woman come in the store, walk down the handicapped ramp, and go between two shelves. To the clerk's amazement, this woman grabbed a ham off the shelf and stuffed it up her dress. With the ham wedged between her thighs, the woman waddled toward the door.

The clerk was stunned and wondered what she should do. Should she yell out? Follow the woman? Just then, the ham dropped out from between the woman's legs. It hit the metal handicapped ramp with a loud bang, and then rolled down it to the bottom.

The shoplifter didn't miss a beat. She quickly turned her head and yelled out, "Who threw that ham at me? Who threw that ham at me?" Then she ran out of the store.

Let this silly, but true, story be a reminder to give up excuses about being too busy. You can no longer innocently ask, "Who stole our time together?" You can no longer wonder how you got "so busy." You made choices. And if you don't own up to them, the time bandits will keep ripping you off.

For Reflection

1. In what specific ways has technology—those electronic gizmos designed to save us more time—ended up stealing yours? Do they sometimes delude you into thinking you're saving time for your marriage when just the opposite is happening? If so, how?

2. When are you most likely to become impatient and why? Can you think of a time when your impatience actually ended up costing you more time than you thought it might save you? What can you learn from that incident?

3. Do you agree that unfinished business from your past can steal time from your present? What have you done to bring closure to unfinished business in your own life?

Workbook Exercise:
Beating Back Your Time Bandits

Both you and your spouse can find this optional workbook exercise in *Your Time-Starved Marriage Workbook* (*for Men/for Women*). Workbooks are available separately at your local bookstore or online at *www.RealRelationships.com*.

Choices. That's what stealing back your time comes down to. This workbook exercise will help you zero in on some specific choices in your situation that may be some of the best you can ever make to regain moments together you've been missing.

---

part 3

the three time mines where you're sure to strike gold

"If you don't know the technique of panning," said seventy-something Irby Hosea, "you lose more gold than you find." According to Irby, he's been prospecting for gold in California most of his life. "The older I get, the colder the river water seems, but I still love it."

We met Irby at the Knott's Berry Farm Amusement Park, where our little boy was trying his hand at panning for gold. We're not sure if it was his "technique" or not, but after several minutes of trying, little John seemed to come up empty. "That's okay," he told us, "it was fun just to try it."

John's a good sport, but I (Les) have to admit that I was a bit disappointed. After all, it's an amusement park where you're buying a ticket for, well, amusement. And I thought finding some gold would certainly be more amusing than not finding it. I mean, you'd think they might hook a little fella up with a nugget or two — even if they're only pebbles spray-painted to look like gold.

Well, in this final section of the book, part 3, we want to show you three areas where you are *guaranteed* to strike gold as a couple when it comes to finding more time together. You are about to see why mealtimes, finances, and recreation are surefire places to reclaim moments you may have been missing in your marriage. These three areas are the real McCoy.

8

meals: what's the rush?

We are what we eat.
Ludwig Feuerbach

Last week I met Steve Anderson, a successful venture capitalist in Seattle who happened to have read one of our previous marriage books. "You're Les Parrott, aren't you?" he asked as he reached out his hand and warmly greeted me. "Welcome to Grace's Kitchen," he said.

I had just stepped into an unusual shop in a quasi-industrial section of our city, not far from our home. I'd never even noticed the place until this day. In fact, the only reason I stepped in was to ask directions to another address where I had an appointment.

"Is this a restaurant?" I asked Steve.

"Not exactly. It's a place to get a gourmet meal to enjoy at home," he said proudly as he gave me his calling card.

As I looked around, I realized the whole store was basically a big kitchen with gleaming stainless steel appliances and several pleasant cooks involved in food preparation.

I was intrigued. "Who's Grace?" I asked.

"Grace isn't a person; it's a state of mind."

I was more intrigued. Steve and I talked for several minutes as he told me about the concept of his business venture. "The real intent is to help couples and families slow down around mealtimes and enjoy a tasty little feast that they can linger over." It was apparent that this was more than just a business idea for Steve. He had passion in his voice. "When a couple can enjoy a nice meal together, it brings them closer. Some of the best conversations we ever have are over food."

Steve went on to tell me they offer cooking classes, but the main attraction is the frozen dinners containing all you need for a gourmet dinner you can make in just a few minutes. "Started in our kitchen, finished in yours," reads the sign on the window. Whether it be the polenta lasagna with spicy turkey sausage or the Gorgonzola and walnut ravioli in porcini and shallot sauce, or any of their other intriguing entrées, a couple can enjoy one to their liking for about fifteen dollars (for two). Steve graciously gave me a box to take home: spiced steak tacos in warm tortillas with chimichurri sauce and sweet roasted corn. Trust me, these are not your mother's frozen TV dinners.

I could go on about the mouthwatering food, but what intrigued me most about this place was the concept behind it. "People obviously don't eat at home around a table like they used to," says Steve. "Food has become too convenient to not eat it on the run. But for a couple wanting to slow down their pace for a little while after work and linger around the dinner hour—where it can actually last an *hour*—this is a fresh alternative."

> *Food is the most primitive form of comfort.*
>
> **Sheila Graham**

I couldn't wait to tell Leslie about my discovery of "Grace" and the conversation I had with Steve. When I had this chance encounter, we were already doing research on the chapter you're now reading, so it heightened my interest. And we couldn't help but affirm Steve and his business endeavor as he does his part to help couples slow down and smell the spices. After all, mealtime truly is one of the great gold mines for respite and reprieve after a busy day at work. A quality dinner, unrushed, can prove to be the main refueling point for a couple's connection. That's why we dedicate this chapter to helping you maximize your mealtimes together.

The Sad State of Slow Food

"Can I take your order please?" The voice comes from a small scratchy speaker just outside your driver's side window. You tell the lighted menu board what you want and then you "pull around to the pickup window" where your food, wrapped in colored paper and cardboard, is in a paper bag ready to go. Lickety-split.

Before McDonald's ruled the world, people used to sit around the dinner table, eat leisurely home-cooked meals, and enjoy good conversation. After all, there wasn't any other option. But that all changed in the 1950s when a few iconoclasts and self-made men in Southern California defied conventional opinion and began setting up stands where people could buy food on the go. From their cars. Fast. It wasn't long before the fast-food industry transformed not only our diets but our landscape, economy, workforce, and culture.

Over the last few decades, fast food has infiltrated every nook and cranny of American society. In 1970, Americans spent about $6 billion on fast food; today they spend more than $110 billion. Americans now spend more on fast food than on movies, books, magazines, newspapers, videos, and recorded music — combined.

The McDonald's Corporation is the nation's largest purchaser of beef, pork, and potatoes. It spends more money on advertising and marketing than any other brand. As Eric Schlosser, author of the disturbing *Fast Food Nation*, writes: "The impact of McDonald's on the way we live today is hard to overstate. The Golden Arches are now more widely recognized than the Christian cross."[1]

And its impact on enjoying a slow-paced, home-cooked meal around the dinner table almost goes without saying. In his book *Bowling Alone*, Robert Putman reports that in America over the past twenty-five years, dinners at home have dropped 33 percent.[2]

The Gobble-Gulp-and-Go of Today's Meals

Fast food has become a mere pit stop to keep us going as we move from one activity to another. We often eat it solo while doing something else, like working, driving, reading, or surfing the Net. And even when we eat at home, it's often something like a Hot Pocket or a mug of soup we microwave on the go.

About the same time the drive-through was being born in Southern California, Swanson unveiled the first TV dinner—a highly processed, all-in-one platter containing turkey with corn-bread dressing and gravy, sweet potatoes, and buttered peas. And not long after that, another culinary time-saver made its debut: instant rice. Uncle Ben got in on the idea by promising housewives "long-grain rice that's ready in ... five minutes!"

In the 1970s, cooking at home moved from being measured in minutes to being timed in seconds. With the introduction of the microwave oven, the original Swanson's TV dinner that took twenty-five minutes to cook in a conventional oven now seemed painfully slow.

Somewhere in the mid-1950s, food became less about its flavor and nutritional value and more about how little time it took to make. Cooking, it was decided, was a chore that didn't deserve our time. And in the rush to speed through the kitchen or bypass it altogether, the intrinsic relational value of a home-cooked meal was unwittingly lost.

What a Real Meal Will Do for Your Marriage

When you allow the fast-food mentality to infiltrate the majority of your meals, you are missing out on one of the very best means to reclaiming the moments you've been missing together. Why? Because a leisurely meal gives a couple an oasis of slowness and a way to rejoin their spirits. Think about it. What happens in your relationship when the two of you step off the treadmill to actually sit down without a scheduled appointment nipping at your heels? A meal where you don't hear or say things like: "We've got to order fast," or "We don't have time for dessert," or "We've got to eat quickly," or "Where's our waitress?" A slow meal occurs when you allow your souls to catch up and be reunited after a fast-paced day.

We recently celebrated our twentieth wedding anniversary. And like most couples, one of the ways we marked this milestone was with a fancy meal—just the two of us. But this was like no meal we had ever experienced. We arrived at the five-star Herbfarm in the foothills of the Cascade Mountains at six o'clock, and the meal did not end until well after eleven o'clock. No entertainment, no interludes, just five leisurely hours of a nine-course meal. Occasionally we'd take a walk around the gardens in between courses, but most of our time was spent talking about anything and everything that came to mind. Talk about having time to let your souls catch up! With our two boys safe at home with a babysitter, we relished the slow pace of the evening. We basked in the time we had with no agenda other than to be together.

Granted, this is not the kind of meal we'd want all the time. It was highly unusual, to say the least. But it underscored for us the value "slow food" brings to our relationship. Truth is, a slow approach to food strengthens any relationship. There is something in the nature of eating together that forms a bond between people.

Sharing food with another human being is an intimate act that should not be indulged in lightly.

M. F. K. Fisher

As Carl Honoré points out in his book *In Praise of Slowness*, "It is no accident that the word 'companion' is derived from the Latin words meaning 'with bread.'"[3] Meals become meaningful when we share them with our spouse.

Dining together relaxes our spirits and makes us more loving. As playwright Oscar Wilde once said, "After a good dinner one can forgive anybody, even one's own relations."

The Ingredients of a Slow-Cooked Conversation

The menu is beside the point when it comes to the kind of meal we're talking about. It doesn't matter if you're eating roasted sea bass or macaroni and cheese. What does matter is that you're taking your time. The point of sharing the meal together is to recoup the energy you've spent during your day and begin to channel it into your relationship by reconnecting.

Of course, the season of your family life will often dictate how well you pull off a "slow-cooked conversation." If you spend much of your mealtime getting your four-year-old to eat a couple of green beans, for example, we know how you feel. Little ones will challenge your attempts at a meaningful meal. But you don't have to abandon the idea altogether. In fact, with a six-year-old and a two-year-old around our own dinner table, we've decided that what works best for us on occasion is a later meal, just the two of us, after our two boys are tucked into bed. Of course, a teenager's schedule can also hamstring your dinners together. All this to say, if you have children, we know it's a challenge, but what we are about to share with you can still work.

Here are four practical ways to make your slow-food meals more meaningful.

Savor Your Time as Much as Your Meal

Believe it or not, there is actually an official "Slow Food" movement. It began in 1986 when McDonald's opened a restaurant beside the famous Spanish Steps in Rome, Italy. For the locals, this fast-food step crossed the line, and Carlo Petrini, a culinary writer, began a campaign. He wanted to defend good taste, and he said it would "begin at the table of Slow Food."[4]

> **Good food ends with good talk.**
>
> Geoffrey Neighor

Savoring food is easier when you slow down and pay attention to it. And the same is true of your marriage. You will savor your marriage when you slow down and pay attention to your partner. The point is that you cannot take this time for granted. It is precious. Time will float by imperceptibly when you are savoring the moments you have as you share a meal.

Ask the Right Questions

We can't tell you how many times we've heard a wife say to us, "He never has anything to say." She'll tell us how they will go out for an evening together, and over dinner or a cup of coffee "he just sits there." If this describes some of the moments in your marriage, take heart. First, you're not alone. And second, there's an easy solution.

Research shows us that men say three times as many words in public as they do in private. Women, on the other hand, say three times as many words in private as they do in public. So let's be honest: relative to women, men tend to clam up when the conversation is one-on-one. Of course, this is not always the case. These differences can go both ways. But if one of you is more quiet than the other, you can typically find a freer flow of conversation over your mealtimes when each of you is asking the right questions. Namely, "How are you doing?" When you ask this simple question—and mean it—you'll be amazed at the discussion it starts.

So often, we sit down with our sweetheart and want to tell them everything about us. And there's nothing wrong with that, as long as you're just as interested in your partner as you are in yourself. Your spouse may "never have anything to say," because your focus is on *you* (and what you want him to say) rather than on *him*.

When we wrote our book *Love Talk*, we also put together a little follow-up book called *Love Talk Starters* (see *www.RealRelationships. com*). It's not the kind of book you read through. Rather, you thumb through it. Each page has an intriguing question to help you jump-start a conversation. We only mention it here because we know that many couples find it helpful to leave the book right on their kitchen table where they can pick it up to explore a topic together at dinnertime.

Avoid Unpleasantness

Augustine, the early Christian church father, encouraged conversation at meals—but with a strictly enforced rule that the character of an absent person should never be negatively discussed. He even had a warning to this effect carved on a plaque attached to his table.

Not a bad idea. Not the plaque, but the rule.

A final suggestion for maximizing your slow meal together is to decide in advance what you won't talk about. We have some friends who have agreed never to talk about work at the dinner table. The famed Kennedy family had a rule never to talk about money at the family dinner table.

You get the idea. Consider those topics in your relationship that are likely to lead to an unproductive conversation. Maybe it's an issue involving in-laws. Maybe it has to do with paying bills or a project that never seems to end. Or maybe it's a character trait that drives one of you nuts. Whatever

Let not the sands of time get in your lunch.

Deteriorata

the topic, recognize that it's going to impair the kind of conversation you'd like to have as you enjoy your mealtime together, and stay clear of it.

Say Grace

As a kid growing up in Boston (Les), our family would sometimes visit the quaint town of Stockbridge, Massachusetts, home of Norman Rockwell. In fact, on one visit we actually met the famed painter and toured his studio. That's where I saw the original of a print we had in our home. It depicted a nicely dressed elderly woman with her grandson, huddled together on the corner of a table about to have lunch in a crowded restaurant. They both have their heads bowed reverently and their hands are clasped in front of them. They're sharing the other side of the table with two young bucks, one of whom has a cigarette dangling from his mouth, and they're observing the woman and boy as if they'd never seen two people pray before. The title of the painting is "Saying Grace." And it's a graphic reminder of the dignity and beauty of this hallowed tradition.

Chances are you already pray a word of thanks before your meals. Millions of people do. If so, be mindful of why you do this. Don't allow it to become meaningless. And if it's been awhile since you've genuinely thanked God for your blessings together, this is a great time to do so.

By the way, there's no right or wrong way to say grace. We recently heard of a six-year-old boy who asked if he could say grace at a restaurant. They bowed their heads and he prayed, "God is good. God is great. Thank you for the food, and I would even thank you more if Mom gets us ice cream for dessert. And liberty and justice for all! Amen!"

That'll work. The best prayers are generally unscripted and come straight from the heart. Whether it's just the two of you or the whole family, you can never go wrong with a heartfelt word of grace where you pray for one another and the concerns of the day. Prayer is a loving and warm way to start a meal and a great way to join your spirits in thankfulness. Oh, and if it fits your style, don't forget to incorporate a little touch by holding hands while you say grace.

If you're looking for a little guidance in initiating this tradition, here's a common prayer that will help you humbly offer your gratitude:

For food in a world where many walk in hunger,
For friends in a world where many walk alone,
For faith in a world where many walk in fear,
We give you thanks, O Lord. Amen.

Giving Your Mealtimes All You've Got

Ever read or seen the wonderful story by Isak Dinesen called *Babette's Feast*? It's about a strict, dour, fundamentalist community in Denmark. Babette works as a cook for two elderly sisters who have no idea that she once was a chef to nobility back in her native France. Babette's dream is to return to her beloved home city of Paris, so every year she buys a lottery ticket in hopes of winning enough money to return. And every night her austere employers demand that she cook the same dreary meal: boiled fish and potatoes, because, they say, Jesus commanded, "Take no thought of food and drink."

> *If more of us valued food and cheer and song above hoarded gold, it would be a merrier world.*
>
> **J. R. R. Tolkien**

One day the unbelievable happens: Babette wins the lottery! The prize is ten thousand francs, a small fortune. And because the anniversary of the founding of the community is approaching, Babette asks if she might prepare a French dinner for the entire village.

At first the townspeople refuse: "No, it would be sin to indulge in such rich food." But Babette begs them, and finally they relent. But the people secretly vow not to enjoy the feast, believing God will not blame them for eating this sinful meal as long as they do not enjoy it.

Babette begins her preparations. Caravans of exotic food arrive in the village, along with cages of quail and barrels of fine wine.

Finally the big day comes, and the village gathers. The first course is an exquisite turtle soup. While they usually eat in silence, a little conversation begins to emerge with each spoonful of soup.

The atmosphere changes. Someone smiles. Someone else giggles. An arm comes up and drapes over a shoulder. Someone is heard to say, "After all, did not the Lord Jesus say, love one another?" By the time the main entrée of quail arrives, those austere, pleasure-fearing people are giggling and laughing and slurping and guffawing and praising God for their many years together.

This dour group is transformed into a loving community through the gift of a meal. One of the two sisters goes into the kitchen to thank Babette, saying, "Oh, how we will miss you when you return to Paris!" And Babette replies, "I will not be returning to Paris, because I have no money. I spent it all on the feast."[5]

We leave you with this story to remind you that your mealtimes will only be as valuable as you make them. It's not enough to consume slow food if your heart isn't in it. Don't look at this as another task on your to-do list, or you'll miss the point. But if you give it your best, if your head and heart are fully immersed in your mealtime together, time will float by imperceptibly, and you'll wonder why so many couples sacrifice this gold mine of time with a measly meal of fast food.

For Reflection

1. What were mealtimes like at your house as a kid, and how do they differ from what you do today? How has that impacted your time together as a couple versus the kind of time your parents had together?

2. What specific topics would you like to declare as "off limits" around the dinner table? Why?

3. If you could press a magic button to make your mealtimes what you'd like them to be, what would happen? How much

of your ideal could you make a reality by what you bring to
the table—literally?

Workbook Exercise:
Enjoying the Rare Delicacy of Slow Food

Both you and your spouse can find this optional workbook exercise in *Your
Time-Starved Marriage Workbook (for Men/for Women)*. Workbooks are available
separately at your local bookstore or online at *www.RealRelationships.com*.

Do you like to cook together? Or would you both prefer to leave
the cooking to someone else? Discussing these questions and several
others can help you more clearly identify what will help you enjoy
more slow-cooked conversations. And this workbook exercise will
lead you through a series of talking points to do just that.

9

finances: time is money

The highest value in life is found in the stewardship of time.
Robert M. Fine

Would you rather have more money or more time? A little fewer than half of those polled would take the cash.[1] Turns out that 51 percent of us would rather have more free time even if it means less money. And 35 percent of us would rather earn more money even if it means less free time. The rest of us can't quite make up our minds.[2]

The connection between time and money has always been tight. Especially for those in the fast lane. When *Fast Company* magazine asked its readers about the connection, they phrased it this way: If you could have one more hour per day at home or a ten-thousand-dollar a year raise, which would you choose?

It's an interesting query. So how would you answer? Would you rather have an extra hour at home each day or the extra dollars? If you chose the money, you're in the company of the majority of *Fast Company* readers. A whopping 83 percent of them said money, while only 17 percent said they'd take the time at home.[3] This may say more about the readers of *Fast Company* than it does about the general population. Why? Because reams of research over the years have confirmed more often than not that most of the people would take time over money.

Of course, your status and station in life has a lot to do with your values. Anyone with a career and a family is preoccupied with juggling them, to the point where pollsters have found that, given their druthers, most of the jugglers would choose more free time or more flexible hours over more money.

Well, wherever your preference places you, the fact remains that your attitude toward money and how you handle your money plays a major role in marriage, especially as it relates to how much time you have together.

Your Money or Your Wife

"Why do you always make the money decisions?" I asked.

Les and I were standing in the middle of a department store trying to choose a down comforter and a duvet for our bed.

"I don't make the money decisions," he said, "our bank account does."

That remark was followed by a lengthy, shiny discussion—okay, it was a fight—over how we manage, or should manage, our money.

> *My time is as much mine as my money. If I don't let everybody else spend my money, I'm not going to let them spend my time.*
>
> **Fred Smith**

Was *he* in charge or were *we* in charge? Some of our biggest fights are financially focused.

Money, of course, has always provided plenty of fodder for marital discord. It is, after all, the most common source of conflict between couples. And with good reason.

The dollar serves as a weapon of independence. It provides a battleground for disputes over responsibility and judgment. Financial issues can even be a forum for airing doubts about self-worth. A partner who is financially irresponsible, for example, may be broadcasting a message: Rescue me, solve my problems. A spouse's reluctance to accept gifts may hide a deeper lack of trust. A woman who goes on a spending spree every time her husband becomes cold and withdrawn may be trying to get his attention.

The point is that money is a weapon as well as a tool. And if you want to use it to maximize the time you're reclaiming for your marriage, you've got to talk about it. So allow us to ask flat out: How do the two of you manage your money? We realize it's a personal question. Most of us don't like to talk about money. But as you answer this question you may very well discover your finances to be a gold mine for more time together.

Managing Money in Marriage

We're not going to give you the how-tos on money management in this chapter. We're not going to help you construct a budget or show you how to get out of debt. Resources abound on how to do all of that. What we're interested in helping you do is get to the psychology of money from your differing perspectives. Why? Because this is where most couples waste their time when it comes to finances.

> *About the time we think we can make ends meet, somebody moves the ends.*
>
> Herbert Hoover

Take, for example, the role that each of you plays in actually managing your money. Who pays the bills and balances the books? And why? More than half of the married women pay the bills, and three out of five balance the checkbook.

Is one of you in charge of the budget, or do you work on the budget together? Or do you live budget free? Sixty-two percent of men say they're responsible for the family budget, though this may not be as impressive as it sounds. In fact, 85 percent of households either don't have a formal budget or don't stick to the one they've got.

> *As every thread of gold is valuable, so is every moment of time.*
>
> **John Mason**

Nonetheless, it's important to talk about your roles in the process of money management. This includes, by the way, who is the moneymaker. Not so many years ago this went without saying. It was the husband who brought home the bacon. But today, a majority of married couples are dual earners, and 25 percent of women in dual-earner households make more than their husbands.

Exploring your individual roles is the first step toward finding more gold in your personal time mine. The next step comes in realizing and accepting a painful fact.

Working Longer to Spend More = Less Time

Some of us are working longer than we need to because we're spending more money than we need to. Even little items can end up costing quite a bit of work time when you add up the extra work that's required to pay for them.

"Since we live in a culture that says more is better, we derive our sense of importance and status from the quantity of stuff we have," says Allen Bluedorn, professor of management at the University of Missouri. "Consequently, the human motivation mechanism is on the setting of 'more.' That's a formula for personal, social, political, and environmental disaster."[4] It's hard to disagree. We've increased our power to consume but find that all it's producing is more stuff to worry about. So if you're serious about finding more time together, it may be time to go back to *enough*—that pleasurable state of having everything we want but nothing in excess. What do you think? Can you live with merely enough?

It's something to consider. There's no getting around this cold, hard formula: Working Longer to Spend More = Less Time. You can't argue with it. But when having enough becomes the goal, you can strike a balance in your life, giving you time for your relationship.

Which leads us to another misnomer that causes time-conscious couples to stumble.

"Fifty/Fifty" Is a Fallacy

During World War II, economist E. F. Schumacher, then a young statistician, worked on a farm. Each day he would count the thirty-two head of cattle, then turn his attention elsewhere. One day an old farmer told him that if he counted the cattle, they wouldn't flourish. Sure enough, one day he counted only thirty-one; one was dead in the bushes. Now Schumacher understood what the farmer meant: you must watch the quality of each beast. "Look him in the eye. Study the sheen on his coat." You may not know how many cattle you have, but you might save the life of one that is sick.

This is wise counsel for married couples managing money together as well. When we begin to count who is spending how much on what and how often, we place our marriage on a scale. Rather than focusing on building the best marriage, we begin to measure how much each of us is getting out of the marriage. The relationship begins to resemble a bank where we go to withdraw our fair share of the dough rather than to invest whatever we can.

Once this attitude permeates our money management, our together-time is sure to suffer. Time begins to get divvied up like dollars. We begin to count how much time the other person has spent playing golf or talking on the phone, or whatever. The whole relationship becomes a counting game, and we pretend to think we could actually create a fifty-fifty relationship. Well, if you don't know it already, that kind of relationship doesn't exist. And the mere attempt to find it will set you up for a nit-picky relationship of splitting hairs at every turn.

If you happen to fall into this fifty-fifty fallacy, allow us to make a simple suggestion: Stop. We know it's a little blunt, but it's the best way out of this trap. Simply stop counting. Stop thinking in terms of percentages you divvy up. Agree with each other to stop by setting a budget that you both can live with. Give and take to agree where your money will go, and let that settle the issue. Next time one of you begins to weigh percentages, you can let the mutually agreed upon budget do the talking.

> *We think much more about the use of our money, which is renewable, than we do about the use of our time, which is irreplaceable.*
>
> Stephan Rechtchaffen

What, Me Worry?

In chapter 7, "Time Bandits," we talked about how impatience robs us of time in our relationship. Well, worry is another time stealer—especially as it relates to money.

A full 67 percent of Americans are more concerned about their financial security than their physical security. So which money matters keep you up at night? More than half of us fear that at some point, we'll have to scrimp every day just to get by. Another 21 percent fret about outliving retirement savings.[5]

Think of the hours we waste by worrying about money. Obviously, money deserves our attention. It's vital to living in our society.

But when it consumes our thoughts and corrodes our thinking with worry, it's wasting our time.

So what are we saying? Quit worrying about money? Not exactly. But we are saying that you can minimize your financial worries by taking a very practical step—today.

You worry most about running out of money, right? No wonder! Despite our financial fears, only 52 percent of us have money saved up outside of a work-related savings or retirement plan. And what we do save isn't enough: Most of us put away less than 5 percent of our net income into savings and investment vehicles. Seventeen percent of all Americans say they don't put any of their income into investments or savings.

> *Can all your worries add a single moment to your life? Of course not.*
>
> **Matthew 6:27 NLT**

If you want to reclaim more time for your marriage, you can do so by minimizing your financial worries. And you do that by working your way out of debt and then building up your savings. You don't have to be a miser. If you do it right, you'll hardly notice the amount that will be going into your savings. In fact, you will even save time in the process of saving money. How? By doing it automatically.

David Bach, author of *The Automatic Millionaire*, says you must have a system that will pull money out of your paycheck directly and automatically—the way the federal government does. And that's easy to do. Go to your employer and say, "I want you to take money directly out of my paycheck, and I want you to put it automatically into my retirement account." Why does this work? Because if you are like most people, you can't trust yourself to pull that money out. "It's not that people are lazy," says Bach, "it's that they're busy. No matter how disciplined they may be, they don't have time to manually write checks and deposit them into an account every pay day."[6]

So take some worry out of your financial quotient and put some time back into your marital bank account.

Giving What You Can

Religious reformer Martin Luther observed, "There are three conversions necessary: the conversion of the heart, the mind, and the purse." Of the three, the purse can be the most difficult for some couples. Agreeing on money matters is always an emotional proposition, and deciding how much to give away can be especially challenging. But it's a crucial part of your conversation.

Billy Graham once said, "If a person gets his attitude toward money straight, it will help straighten out almost every other area of his life." In other words, once you have a healthy perspective on using your money for good, other things — like time management — tend to fall more easily into place. So as you continue to reclaim your moments together, don't neglect this important discussion. Consider the freedom and joy that comes from making money to give it away. And remember the words of Francis Bacon: "Money is like mulch, not good except it be spread."

Show Me the Time!

The 1996 film *Jerry Maguire* is known for several memorable lines but none more popular than the one uttered by Cuba Gooding Jr.'s character in his Oscar-winning performance as Rod Tidwell, a professional football player desiring and demanding the multimillion-dollar contract the other star players were receiving. He's on the phone to his agent, Jerry Maguire, played by Tom Cruise, when he repeatedly yells: "Show me the money!"

The line became a battle cry for countless employees across the country. "Show me the money!" they demanded of their employers.

"Show me the money, and I'll improve my performance." Years later, the line is just as popular.

Do you think it would have stuck in our collective consciousness if the commodity was time instead of money? Can you imagine Cuba Gooding Jr. shouting, "Show me the time!"? It's a tough sell, isn't it? But the rephrased line is exactly what every time-savvy couple must demand of their money. Remember, time is money. And how you spend it determines the return on your investment.

Minutes are worth more than money. Spend them wisely.

Thomas P. Murphy

For Reflection

1. Would you rather have an extra hour at home each day or an extra ten thousand dollars? Why?

2. What do you think about the idea of living with merely "enough"? What would this mean to the two of you, and is it something you would seriously consider in order to have more time? Why or why not?

3. What's your biggest financial worry right now? How does this worry eat up your time? What is within your power to do within the next twelve months that would reduce this worry significantly? What would keep you from doing this?

Workbook Exercise:
Money Talks and So Can We

Both you and your spouse can find this optional workbook exercise in *Your Time-Starved Marriage Workbook (for Men/for Women)*. Workbooks are available separately at your local bookstore or online at *www.RealRelationships.com*.

Money seems to be a topic most couples fight about more than they talk about. If you're ready to have a reasonable conversation about your finances together and guard yourselves against it becoming tense, we want to help you do just that. This workbook exercise will walk you through one of the most important conversations a time-conscious couple can have.

10

rest: recouping
what you crave

Don't put off 'til tomorrow the siesta you can take today.
Thierry Paquot

Aristotle, that canny Greek philosopher, said long ago that we humans work in order to have leisure. It's a little like dieting so you can eat again. We work a lot, we rest a little. Then we work some more to enjoy a little more leisure. Trouble is, our rest time seems to be shrinking. When was the last time you literally did nothing?

G. K. Chesterton suggested that what Aristotle meant by leisure was not simply inertia, doing nothing at all, but rather, doing something different from our usual tasks in life, doing something that we wanted to do for itself, doing something that gave us joy that was not part of the work life. In other words, true leisure is rejuve-

> *To be able to fill leisure intelligently is the last product of civilization.*
>
> **Bertrand Russell**

nating, re-creating, resting, and recovering ourselves. Enjoying rest is not done to be a better worker but, rather, to be a better person — to be a better couple.

Your marriage cannot survive on work alone. Just as the body requires rest, so does your relationship. So we dedicate this final chapter to helping you recoup the downtime you've been missing and maximize it for the sake of your marriage.

Leisure Sickness

Much of the world often scoffs at the tradition of the siesta in Italy, Spain, and Mexico. We smirk at the French practice of closing down in August and Sweden's mandated five-week minimum vacation policy.

Most people in North America and many other places around the globe have never been comfortable with the abstract notion of free time. It is not in our nature to just let time pass. Unstructured time, dead time, downtime, wasted time — it makes us ill at ease. In fact, for some of us, it literally makes us sick.

Consider a typical scenario. The weekend's finally here. You're ready to unwind and relax. But you're headachy, tired, or you've got a stiff neck and maybe are even coming down with the flu. Researchers at Tilburg University in the Netherlands say these symptoms strike perfectionists or people who carry large workloads and feel very responsible at their job. These people are more apt to suffer from these symptoms, termed "leisure sickness," and they have a tough time making the transition from the daily grind to home life.

The Dutch researcher, Ad Vingerhoets, began his study after noticing that some of his own weekends and vacations were spent suffering through headaches and other physical ailments. He tried to find out if any studies had been done on the perplexing phenomenon and found none. So Vingerhoets, whose research area is stress and emotions, decided to study the subject himself.

The researcher and his team observed more than one hundred people who were plagued by headaches, muscle pain, fatigue, and nausea over weekends and holidays. Most of the subjects reported suffering from these symptoms in their downtimes for more than ten years.

There may be other explanations for your leisure sickness, according to the researcher. "You may be more aware of your symptoms in a quiet environment as opposed to the hectic workplace," says Vingerhoets. Or your body could be staving off illness until you can slow down.[1]

The solution? We're getting to that.

Giving It a Rest

Whether you suffer from "leisure sickness" or not, you need to take a break. Unless you are in a very small minority, you rarely feel rested. In a recent phone survey of over a thousand households, the Families and Work Institute discovered that the vast majority of American couples feel overworked. Of those surveyed, 55 percent reported feeling overwhelmed by how much work they have to do, and 90 percent agreed strongly that they work "too hard."[2]

And if workers are discovered to not feel overwhelmed, if they are getting more work done in less time than others, how do we reward them? With rest? Hardly. We figure that if they can balance three spinning plates on three thin sticks, they should be given a fourth plate. Then a fifth.

Another survey conducted by the Families and Work Institute of New York concluded that both spouses in a double-income household with kids each put in a minimum of fifteen hours a day on work, commuting, chores, and children.[3] These figures, based on a Monday-through-Friday schedule, mean that each spouse has already "logged in" seventy-five hours before the weekend. Moreover, Saturdays for many have become just another workday. We draw up "honey-do lists," assign chores, attend to projects, and taxi kids to friends, activities, and the mall.

Couples are working harder and longer today than ever before. Not only are we spending more time on the job, the tempo and intensity of our workdays has accelerated.

Whew! It's time for a break.

How to Recoup Your Relational R & R ... and R

We used to think our busyness was temporary. A mere season of chaos. "Things will even out soon," we'd tell ourselves. But recent research has shown us that we are no longer swallowing this false assumption. Which would be encouraging if we were doing something about it. But as it turns out, we're simply becoming more complacent, if not more pessimistic in the process. A recent *Newsweek* poll found that 64 percent of those surveyed believe they will have less leisure time in the future than they have now.[4]

If that describes you, we've got encouraging words. You don't have to slave away without recharging your batteries. You don't have to work like a mule that never takes a break. You can quit your job! Too drastic? Okay. We have another alternative. It involves a revised version of the three Rs:

- Rest
- Recreation
- Restoration

If you believe you do not have enough time to practice these three Rs, you have just proven how badly you need them. This morning, millions of people got up before dawn and went to work. Many because they had to, some because they wouldn't have it any other way. It's this latter group that poet Thomas Carlisle was considering when he wrote, "Blessed is he who has found his work; let him ask no other blessedness, he has a work, a life-purpose." John Gardner, leader of the Washington-based think tank, Common Cause, echoed this sentiment when he said, "What can be more satisfying than to be engaged in work in which every capacity or talent one may have is needed, every lesson one may have learned is used, every value one cares about is furthered?" Carlisle and Gardner are indeed right. Work can be a calling, a true blessing that brings fulfillment. But for others it is a curse, a mere means to survival. Wherever you are on that continuum, whether you are the founder and CEO of a successful corporation or an hourly wage earner at a faceless factory or a stay-at-home parent with active toddlers, you—and your marriage—can benefit from practicing these three Rs.

Rest: Taking Time for Sweet, Sweet Slumber

At the end of many entries in his famous diaries depicting the early Restoration period in England, Samuel Pepys signed off with an endearing phrase: "And so to bed."

For Pepys, those four little words marked the end of another day in seventeenth-century London. In today's world, the phrase could serve as a clever rallying cry for a fledgling movement that wants to encourage people to catch more z's.

At one time, new parents constituted the primary group of sleep-deprived adults. Now two-thirds of Americans don't get eight hours of sleep every night, according to the National Sleep Foundation. The result, the group says, is a nation of sleepyheads.

In our demanding 24/7 world, sleep has become expendable, even a waste of time. To admit to getting a full night's sleep is to risk characterizing oneself as a dullard. The new form of bragging has become: "I'm too busy and important to sleep."

Have you fallen for this delusion? Make no mistake—it's a lie. We all need sleep. It's not a luxury. People from every part of the world, hippos in the jungle, fish in aquariums—they all sleep! Sleep is as important as breathing or eating. In fact, people can survive longer without food than they can without sleep.

Without adequate sleep, our bodies pay a serious price. We become sluggish in our thinking. Irrational. Irritable. Our reaction times slow down. We become more vulnerable to illness. A sleep debt of three to four hours each night per week can lead to hormone imbalances. People who don't sleep enough have trouble concentrating and figuring out logical problems. They're more likely to fall prey to feelings of sadness, depression, and anger, and their immune systems can become compromised. We even age more quickly and gain weight more easily without adequate sleep.

How beautiful it is to do nothing, and then rest afterward.

Spanish Proverb

Experts tell us we require about eight hours of sleep to function at our best. Yet one-third of adults report they normally sleep less than six and a half hours a night. And even those hours are not always restful. Which means we're not reaching our "dream quotient."

Dreams, those mystical fantasies of slumber, are often bizarre and we can't always make much sense of them. But with enough sleep, everybody dreams. A normal night's sleep always includes not one but several periods of dreaming. Research studies have established this beyond any doubt. The question for years has been, what do these dreams do? Today's experts are finding answers. During dream sleep, the brain consolidates memory, clears our unresolved issues, and helps us forget things we don't need to remember. The brain, like the hard drive on your computer, needs cleaning up from time to time. That is what dream sleep does for the mind.

So here's the key to a good night's sleep: You have to get enough dream sleep to achieve the benefits. If you only sleep for six hours, you will be missing out on several major periods of dreaming and will not be getting enough dream sleep. So do what you can, together, to get the sleep you need, not just for your body, but for your mind too.

Here's your assignment: Have some pillow talk tonight about how you can help each other become better sleepers. It may sound strange, but as you help each other become more rested, you and your relationship will operate at the optimum level. Think of all the needless conflicts you can avoid (and time you will save). Here are a few suggestions to get you started: getting to bed consistently at the same time each night, exercising at some point in the day, not snacking late at night, giving each other a gentle back rub before dozing off, and so on. The point is to get serious about your sleep and discuss specific ways that each of you can help the other sleep better — starting tonight.

Recreation: Getting Serious about Having Fun

"I'm constantly amazed by the number of people who can't seem to control their own schedules," says legendary businessman Lee Iacocca. "Over the years, I've had many executives come to me and say with pride, 'Boy, last year I worked so hard that I didn't take any vacation.' It's actually nothing to be proud of. I always feel like responding, 'You dummy. You mean to tell me you can take responsibility for an $80 million project, and you can't plan two weeks out of the year to go off with your family and have some fun?'"[5]

> *Work expands so as to fill the time available for its completion.*
>
> C. Northcote Parkinson

He makes a good point, don't you think? Having fun is what recreation is all about. We need to make a space on our jam-packed calendar to get away from the rigors and responsibilities of the job, to unwind, change our pace, and temporarily sever our ties to work. At least that's what vacation is intended to do.

A survey by Management Recruiters International Inc., the world's largest search and recruitment organization, shows that a mind-boggling 82 percent of our vacations include bringing work with us.[6] Seems these days we're more inclined to have a "working vacation." Can you believe it? We're spoiling our vacations by phoning the office and emailing colleagues. On top of that, 13 percent of us admit to shortening our vacations once we are on them because of work.[7]

And it's not just vacations that are getting bamboozled by work. Seems our weekends are also at risk. Less than a quarter of people today associate weekends with having fun. A poll of more than a thousand women revealed that one in seven find the weekend is a time when depression sets in about the week ahead.[8]

Half our life is spent trying to find something to do with the time we have rushed through life trying to save.

Will Rogers

Yikes! It's time we got serious about having fun. That's exactly what Ken and Stacy Coleman have done. This Atlanta couple is one of the most fun-loving couples we know. In their early thirties, Ken and Stacy work hard. They're both go-getters who live in the fast lane. But they know when to cool their jets. They've nearly perfected the fine art of playing together, and they aren't about to blur the boundaries between work and play. They begin each year by inking their calendar with the days they will devote to vacationing and recreation. Last year one of the highlights was a Caribbean cruise that they scrimped and saved for. But it's not their vacations that impress us. They know how to squeeze every ounce of fun out of a weekend — those weekly minivacations too many of us fill with more work.

"I leave my least taxing projects for Friday afternoon," Ken told me, "so I can ease my way into the weekend." He went on to say that if he's dealing with a major project right up to quitting time on Friday, it's bound to contaminate the time they've set aside for fun. "It doesn't matter what we're doing come Friday night," says Stacy, "but I know we're not going to be talking about work. Friday evening marks the beginning of a conscious effort to be fully present for whatever we decide would be a blast." This is a couple that places a priority on their recreation as well as their work. This is a couple who's striking that proverbial balance we all desire.

How do they and other couples do it? Ken suggests beginning with a ritual. "Some time ago we splurged on a massage chair that sits in the corner of our bedroom, and twenty minutes in that chair signals the start of the weekend for me." Other couples begin their weekend ritual by exercising together. Whatever the marker, find some way to highlight the change from workweek to weekend.

> *A vacation is what you take when you can no longer take what you've been taking.*
>
> **Earl Wilson**

In addition, we urge you to find an activity you can enjoy together in your time off work. Do this and you'll notice a measurable degree of increased satisfaction in your weekends. This is critically important for husbands. Willard Harley says, "Spending recreational time with his wife is second only to sex for the typical husband." It's true. One of the great gaps between husbands and wives is found in their notions of emotional intimacy. For most women, intimacy means sharing secrets, talking things over, cuddling, and so on. But a man builds intimacy differently. He connects by doing things together. Working in the garden or going to a movie with his wife gives him a feeling of closeness. Husbands place surprising importance on having their wives as recreational companions.

So don't neglect this important aspect of your weekend, your vacation, or wherever you can make the time to share an activity you both enjoy. Think of your fun time together as your insurance policy against the fading of passion and intimacy in your relationship. You'll find a list of potential activities to share with your partner on our website at *www.RealRelationships.com.*

Restoration: Making Your Sabbath a Retreat for Your Soul

In Nan Fink's memoir *Stranger in the Midst*, she describes the preparations she and her husband made for their traditional Jewish Sabbath:

> On Friday afternoon, at the very last minute, we'd rush home, stopping at the grocery to pick up supplies. Flying into the kitchen we'd cook ahead for the next twenty-four hours. Soup and salad, baked chicken, yams and applesauce for dinner, and vegetables or lasagna for the next day's lunch. Sometimes I'd think how strange it was to be in such a frenzy to get ready for a day of rest.
>
> Shabbat preparations had their own rhythm, and once the table was set and the house straightened, the pace began to slow. "It's your turn first in the shower," I'd call to Michael. "Okay, but it's getting late," he'd answer, concerned about starting Shabbat at sunset.

In the bathroom I'd linger at the mirror, examining myself, stroking the little lines on my face, taking as much time as I could to settle into a mood of quietness. When I joined Michael for the lighting of the candles, the whole house seemed transformed. Papers and books were neatly piled, flowers stood in a vase on the table; and the golden light of the setting sun filled the room....

Shabbat is like nothing else. Time as we know it does not exist for these twenty-four hours, and the worries of the week soon fall away. A feeling of joy appears. The smallest object, a leaf or a spoon, shimmers in a soft light, and the heart opens. Shabbat is a meditation of unbelievable beauty.[9]

The full Hebrew custom of Shabbat is difficult to incorporate into the Christian life, but the Sabbath is a basic unit of Christian time, a day the church also tries to devote to reverence for God and rest from toil. And yet, if we are not intentional, our holy day of going to church for worship can

> *Remember the Sabbath day by keeping it holy.*
>
> **Exodus 20:8**

become just another activity on our busy calendar. Without intention, time continues to exist like every other day.

God first commands the Sabbath to the Jewish people in Exodus, with the initial revelation of the Ten Commandments, and then again in Deuteronomy. Perhaps because of this, it's easy to look at the Jewish Sabbath as a long list of thou shalt nots: Don't turn on lights, don't drive, don't cook, don't plan for the week ahead, and so on. What all this boils down to (and boiling is another thing you cannot do on Shabbat) is: Do not create. For one of the things the Sabbath reprises is God's rest after he finished creating. The point being that if God rested, we can too. As Moishe Konigsberg says, "When we don't operate machines, or pick flowers, or pluck fish from the sea ... when we cease interfering in the world, we are acknowledging that it is God's world."

Are we suggesting that Christians embrace the strict regulations of the Orthodox Jewish Sabbath? No. The New Testament unambiguously inaugurates a new understanding of Shabbat.[10] In his epistles, Paul makes clear that Sabbath observance, like other external signs of piety, is insufficient for salvation.[11] But there is something in the Jewish Sabbath that is absent from most Christian Sundays: a true cessation from the rhythms of work and world, a time wholly set apart. Sunday is not meant to be just an add-on to our week. Sunday is our holy day of rest—"set apart" from the other days. When we fail to live a Sabbath truly distinct from weekly time, we are missing out on one of the greatest means God has given us to find rest—rest in him.[12]

So we ask: How are you keeping the Sabbath? Are you refraining from working, mowing lawns, balancing checkbooks? If so, good for you. If not, you're more like us. By Sunday evening in our house you can feel the workweek creeping in. But we're doing our best to set this day apart and keep it holy. We do more than merely attend church and eat a leisurely brunch. We take a walk. We talk. We read. It's not much, but it has more to do with what we don't do than what we do. We don't go shopping. We don't churn out email or return calls. We don't channel surf. Although we're not always consistent, we're doing our best to set Sunday apart from the other days in our week in an attempt to replenish our souls, renew our spirits, and remember our Creator.

The time you enjoy wasting is not wasted time.

Bertrand Russell

Henri J. Nouwen, in his book, *The Road to Daybreak*, said, "I feel a tension within me. I have only a limited number of years left.... Why not use them well? Time given to inner renewal is never wasted. God is not in a hurry." Whenever we find ourselves feeling as though we're not being productive, when we are tempted to think that our Sabbath is stealing time from what we could be doing to get ahead, we try to remember what Nouwen said. Inner renewal is never wasted.[13]

Sabbath-keeping couples are a minority in a world that often encourages commerce twenty-four hours a day, seven days a week. We won't kid you, it takes discipline to forsake some work on the side, whether it be related to the office or a much-needed household chore. But if you're serious about reclaiming more moments for your time-starved marriage, you won't find a more God-given gift for recouping the rest your relationship craves than that of keeping the Sabbath day holy.

For Reflection

1. How much sleep do you normally get each night? Is it enough? If not, what would allow you to get the sleep your body craves? Be specific.
2. What's the most fun recreational activity you enjoy as a couple when you have the time for it? What other activities do you enjoy together and how can you, in specific terms, create more time to enjoy them?
3. What's the typical "Sabbath" like in your home? Are you doing everything you'd like to make it a true retreat for your soul? Identify one specific action you could take this coming week that would improve it.

Workbook Exercise:
Getting Real about R & R

Both you and your spouse can find this optional workbook exercise in *Your Time-Starved Marriage Workbook (for Men/for Women)*. Workbooks are available separately at your local bookstore or online at *www.RealRelationships.com*.

In this final workbook exercise, we help you get serious about having more fun. In addition to enjoying more recreating, however, we want to help you rest your weary body and restore your soul. We want to help you replenish the three Rs: Rest, Recreation, and Restoration. This exercise will walk you through a way of doing just that.

conclusion

as time goes by

And what if you were told: One more hour?
Elia Canetti

On a shelf in our garage is a large can of the popular lubricant WD–40. It's been there for years, literally. Every time we pull in to park the car we see that large blue and gold can, used for stopping squeaks. Some time ago as the electric garage door was closing behind us, Leslie asked me what WD–40 stood for. Interesting question. I'd never thought about it. And I had no idea. That was that.

But as the weeks went by, I kept seeing that spray can and wondering, *Why* would *they call it that?* There's certainly nothing catchy about the name. Did they consult a marketing company? Does the "40" stand for how many months it lasts? Why "WD"? I studied the can, read all the small print. Nothing. It began to eat at me. I had to know what was behind this name. I asked some of my buddies. They were clueless. And didn't seem to care. *How could you not be curious?* I thought to myself. Was I losing it over a simple can of lubricant? For whatever reason, I *had* to know the answer to this innocent question Leslie had posed.

Then it hit me. I should try the Internet. The tool I use for research nearly every day would certainly reveal the answer. So I Googled "WD–40" and tracked down their website. That's when I

133

discovered a delightful animated can of lubricant squirting everything from engines to snow shovels. I learned that WD–40 "cleans, protects, penetrates, lubricates, and displaces moisture like no other product on earth." I learned that it comes in more sizes than I could imagine, and that it even comes in a "professional grade." Its headquarters are in San Diego, and it's sold in more than 160 countries. I learned that "consumers have had a love affair with WD–40." In fact, consumers are so wild about WD–40, that, according to their website, "there was only one thing to do—compile a list of two thousand uses and start an official WD–40 Fan Club!"[1]

I'm serious. They have a place to sign up, enter a passcode, and begin receiving the WD–40 Newsletter. You can also opt to receive the weekly e-tip on using the lubricant. And, I kid you not, there's a place for you to read and write stories about the product's use. If you like what you're reading, you can "tell a friend" with just a click of your mouse. Or do the same thing and make the lubrication site your home page.

I like the product enough to have a can in my garage, but I had no idea that some people—people I've never met in real life—are fanatical about this stuff. I simply wanted to conclude my quest to discover why the taunting blue and gold can has such a ridiculously vague and abstract name.

And yet, with all the seemingly endless information about their product on their website, there was not a peep about why it was called WD–40.

Well, my long and arduous quest came to a conclusion when I stopped in a locally owned hardware store on top of Queen Anne Hill in Seattle. That's where Frank, the longtime owner, told me that he sells dozens of cans of this stuff every week.

your time-starved marriage

"Do you know why they call it 'WD–40'?" I asked nonchalantly, expecting him to shrug his shoulders.

"Sure," Frank said. "It stands, if I'm not mistaken, for 'water displacement.'"

"What?" I yelped. "You can't be serious! Then what does the '40' refer to?"

"Well," he said, "that's how many times they tried to develop an effective formula. They failed thirty-nine times but succeeded on the fortieth try."

"Really?" Now that *was* interesting to me. In finding the right concoction, it took thirty-nine attempts before getting it right. That means somebody didn't give up along the way. You've got to admire that. At least I do. WD–40. *What a great name*, I thought. Turns out the name came straight out of the lab book used by the chemist, Norm Larsen, back in 1953.

The name's cryptic, no doubt, but it certainly stands for something once you know the story behind it. In fact, it's hard to get the message out of your mind.

I now think of Norm's perseverance nearly every time I spy that blue and gold can in our garage. Leslie does too. In fact, that can of protectant has become a symbol for us in our marriage.

We know this sounds silly, but every marriage needs a figurative can of WD–40 around as a reminder to keep trying. Even after practicing all the tips and exercises we've given you in this book, after doing all that you can to reclaim the moments you've been missing in your time-starved marriage, you are going to have occasions where you feel like you're stuck, like you can't break the cycle of your breakneck schedule. Don't be discouraged in these moments. Try again. Don't give up. Your time together is too valuable, too glorious, to surrender. Time keeps moving forward, but your love, as the song says, is "never out of date" because:

The world will always welcome lovers
As time goes by.[2]

appendix

your personal time-style combinations

How to Use This Appendix

In chapter 4 you learned about your personal time style — whether you are primarily an Accommodator, Dreamer, Planner, or Processor. Accurately understanding your style and your partner's, as well as the dynamic relationship between them, will help you maximize the moments you spend together.

The online Time-Style Marriage Assessment at *www.Real Relationships.com* will provide a personalized report on your two time styles, helping you more accurately determine into which category you and your partner fall. In addition, this appendix will help you better understand how your two styles are likely to interact, both positively and negatively.

This appendix is not meant to be read in its entirety. Instead, peruse the list of categories below. Match up your time style with your partner's time style. Then turn to the page that pertains to your combination and read the section that is relevant to you. Your partner can do the same. And unless you both fall into the same style category (e.g., you're both Planners), you will be reading different pages. As you zero in on your two time styles, you will learn how they affect your interaction as a couple.

No matter what category you fall into, we wish you the best as you work to maximize your moments together.

If You're an Accommodator Married to a Dreamer

As a person who approaches time subjectively, you tend to be relatively unscheduled. And so does your partner. You both enjoy an experiential, more intuitive, relationship with time. But the two of you focus your energy in different places.

While you focus primarily on the present, your partner focuses primarily on the future. And as you are probably already aware, this can sometimes cause conflict. After all, while you are living in the here and now, your spouse is thinking about what's down the road—or maybe even considering what road to take, or even build. As a Dreamer, your partner resonates with the statement by Henry David Thoreau: "Go confidently in the direction of your dreams. Live the life you have imagined."

You, on the other hand, as an Accommodator, would be more likely to amend this quote to read something along the lines of: "Go with the flow in the present moment. Live the life that is happening right now."

So what does this mean for how you manage time as a couple? First of all, you are likely to lose meaningful time together whenever you attempt to convert your partner to be more present oriented. Save your breath. Your partner is hardwired for the future. But this doesn't mean you have to live there too. In fact, as you gently focus your energy on the here and now, you will tend to pull your partner into the present with you. In other words, coercion will not gain you any more meaningful minutes together.

Also, you'll discover that whenever you can enter your partner's dreaming, your spirits will be joined together. Why? Because this is where your partner comes alive. So while you may not feel naturally inclined to focus on the future, if you will try to do so a little, you will find that these are moments when you are most connected.

Keep in mind that neither of you is all that precise when it comes to time. You both tend to be more "unscheduled" than "scheduled." This can work in your favor as long as you are not expecting your partner to make up for something you don't do. For example, you may struggle to meet deadlines (e.g., paying the bills, completing a project) and so may your partner. As a couple, therefore, this means you may not always get done what you would like to—and most of the time, that's probably alright with both of you. But you're bound to run into times when that can be frustrating. Don't waste time blaming your partner about this. You're in the same subjective boat of timekeeping.

You're also both inclined to be spontaneous and relatively unscheduled. This means that some of your best times together are not likely to be planned. That's a good thing. But you may benefit from making a few more plans together in your schedules. Think of them, not as appointments, but as healthy rituals or routines.

Things to keep in mind:

- You may tend to get frustrated with your partner "always thinking about tomorrow." Try to enter this dreaming as best you can whenever you can.
- Don't be a downer by trying to talk your partner out of dreaming. You'll get further by gently living in the present than by coercing your partner to join you.
- You're both more "unscheduled" than "scheduled." This means some of your best times together are going to be spontaneous.
- You can benefit from doing a smidge more planning to protect your times together.

If You're an Accommodator Married to a Planner

When it comes to your two time styles, you're in what is sometimes known as a complementary relationship. Your subjective approach to time complements your partner's objective experience, and vice versa. The same is true when it comes to where each of you puts your energy. You are present oriented, and this complements your partner's future orientation. So on both dimensions of time—how you experience it and where you focus your energy—you are complementary.

Of course, you may be tempted to say you are "opposite" instead of "complementary," and you'd be right. It's another way of saying that your differing time styles can either work for you or against you. It all depends on your attitude and your understanding.

For example, as an Accommodator, you may sometimes love the way your partner goes about planning your life together (e.g., scheduling and preparing for enjoyable experiences), since this is something you are not naturally inclined to do. At other times, however, this planning may get on your nerves. After all, you enjoy a more freewheeling, spontaneous approach to living. You may actually see a plan as interfering with what might more naturally develop. And that's the rub.

So what can you do as an Accommodator married to a Planner to ensure you have more meaningful time together that's enjoyable to both of you? To begin, let your partner plan. That may not sit too well with you all of the time, but that's how your partner is hardwired for time. Your partner is a Planner, so learn to appreciate it. Affirm your partner's more objective and future-oriented style. Recognize how your partner's planning benefits you and your relationship.

If your partner's planning tends to take the spontaneity out of your relationship, however, don't be afraid to rock the boat a bit by disrupting "the plan" with some impulsive fun. Remind your partner that the point is not to fulfill the plan but to enjoy a deeper connection. Use fun-loving humor, not force, when doing this.

Also, recognize how your lack of planning can sometimes drive your partner nuts. Owning your accommodating time style and recognizing its downside will go a long way in helping your partner appreciate it. The more you own it (by making fun of your relatively carefree style, for example), the less anxious your partner will feel about your lack of planning. This will help both of you move more toward a middle ground in some situations and use the best each of you has to offer.

Things to keep in mind:

- You may tend to feel irritated with your partner's detailed plans. But if you accept the fact that being a spontaneous Accommodator isn't always the most helpful style, your irritation will diminish.
- Your partner's anxiety is lowered by making plans for the future. Affirm what this objective approach does for your relationship. Express your appreciation for it.
- Your "unscheduled" approach may be just as irritating to your partner as his or her "scheduled" approach is to you. The more you let your partner know you recognize this in yourself, the more it becomes a nonissue.
- Your styles can either complement each other, pulling you together as you appreciate them, or pull you apart. The choice is yours.

If You're an Accommodator Married to a Processor

Since you are more inclined to experience time subjectively, you tend to be more unscheduled than your partner. As you are already aware, this can occasionally cause tension. However, both of you tend to focus your energy on the present, rather than the future. This keeps you both on the same page of your shared timeline.

As an Accommodator, your freewheeling approach to time can seem like an enigma to your partner. He or she may simply marvel at your more relaxed approach or he or she may become perturbed by it. Either way, your partner probably doesn't understand it, just as you don't always understand your partner's approach. After all, as a Processor, your partner likes to have things nailed down. While you are fine with a few loose ends, closure is crucial to him or her. While your speed can vary as you shift gears to correlate to your mood, your partner likes to keep humming along at an even pace. While you shoot from the hip, your partner tends to aim carefully.

How does all this impact your relationship, and what can you do to use it to your advantage? For starters, you will gain much if you learn to appreciate your partner's "procedures." Sure, they may drive you nuts, but his or her process for doing various activities has its reasons — at least to your partner. So find out what those reasons are. They may not make much sense to you, but take a "that's interesting" approach and you'll begin to understand how your partner is hardwired. Stay clear of a condemning attitude. Simply seek to understand.

Also, put yourself in your partner's shoes. If the roles were reversed, and you were the Processor in the relationship, how would you feel about being married to an unscheduled Accommodator? What would rub you the wrong way on occasion? If you can talk to your partner about this, you'll find that your mutual understanding and respect for your differing styles increases.

Once you more fully understand your partner's more objective approach to time, the next step is to recognize its value. See what it does for your relationship. You might discover that if your partner weren't a Processor, the two of you wouldn't have as much stability in your relationship.

You both can benefit from thinking a bit more about your future. Since you both focus much of your energy on the present, you may be missing good opportunities to recoup time together by dreaming and planning about what's ahead for you. In other words, your relationship would probably improve if both of you got a little more deliberate about charting your course. Where would you like to be in a year's time? What would you like to have experienced or accomplished together? Since you are both in the "here and now" boat together, you can help each other with this task and enjoy a new dimension of your journey.

Things to keep in mind:

- If your partner's "procedures" are getting to you, don't forget to recognize the good that a process brings to your relationship. The more you focus on the positive, the more your irritation will diminish.

- Affirm your partner's approach. Express your appreciation for what a more objective experience of time does for your relationship.

- Own your piece of the pie. Let your partner know that you realize your unscheduled approach can be tough to understand and experience at times.

- Your styles keep you both in the here and now. Don't neglect to plan for your future. Don't disregard the value of dreaming together.

If You're an Accommodator Married to an Accommodator

You're both in the same proverbial boat. Each of you focuses your energy on the present, and each of you experiences time subjectively. So, as two like-minded Accommodators, you're headed in the same direction and it's smooth sailing, right? Well, not exactly.

Two Accommodators married to each other enjoy a freewheeling, spur-of-the-moment, unplanned kind of existence. There's no real need for date books in your relationship, and at times you may be hard-pressed to find your watch. After all, you two can get lost in time. You operate by how it feels more than by what time it is. You each feel comfortable making your way without a relatively structured plan. While you don't ignore the future altogether, it's not nearly as important to you as the present. You certainly make plans, but you're more focused on what's happening right now.

Whether you know it or not, relative to many other couples, you are unique. The future, you reason, will take care of itself. Why worry about it, right? Albert Einstein said, "I never worry about the future, it comes soon enough." You both feel the same way. Good for you. The only problem is that two Accommodators sometimes find out that the future can come knocking on the door sooner than expected. It may come in the form of unpaid bills, unfinished projects, or missed opportunities.

That's the trade-off for traveling through time together without much care. Your lack of planning as a couple can come back to bite you. Of course, your problems can be relatively mild or more serious, depending upon how strong your two Accommodating styles are. The point is that you may benefit from a bit more scheduling and planning. Your finances are a good barometer. If you're feeling no burden or pressure in this department, you've probably learned to accommodate your unscheduled approach. But if you are up to your eyeballs in debt, that's a pretty good indication that your present-oriented time styles need some help. Not only do you probably need a financial advisor (they are Planners and Processors by nature), but also another couple who will mentor you in charting your marital course more deliberately. In other words, a mentor couple might help you structure a way to make sure you are getting the time your relationship deserves and needs. They might help you with a "spending plan" for your time together.

By the way, you two are often gifted at living life fully, so *you* can probably mentor other couples who need some of what you enjoy—especially a couple made up of two Planners! The bottom line is that the two of you have something wonderful in your shared styles. As long as you control your time rather than letting it control you, your relationship will enjoy wonderful moments of unscheduled surprises and happy accidents.

Things to keep in mind:

- Celebrate the shared spontaneity you both bring to your marriage. This is a gift to be enjoyed.
- If your joint time style is keeping you from making productive plans (if you're stuck in a rut), consider what you can do to be more objective and future oriented together.
- What loose ends do each of you need to tie up? Two Accommodators can go far too long without adequately addressing this important topic.
- Consider how another more future-oriented and objective couple might mentor you. What lessons might they teach you (and what might you teach them)?

If You're a Dreamer Married to an Accommodator

Both you and your partner experience time subjectively. This means that you tend to be more unscheduled than scheduled. On the one hand, you both lean toward spontaneity rather than structure. You don't like to feel too confined by a schedule that can tend to put you in a box. On the other hand, you don't necessarily focus your energy in the same direction much of the time. While you are geared to think about the future, your spouse is thinking more about the here and now.

your time-starved marriage

How does this impact your relationship and the time you spend together? For starters, you may sometimes feel like your partner is clipping your wings. After all, you are trying to create an exciting and better tomorrow as you scheme and dream about ways to soar higher in the future. By default, you may perceive your partner's focus on the present as holding you back. This may or may not be true, but generally speaking, it's probably not. It's simply an attempt to help you live in the here and now as you are dreaming about tomorrow. So don't take it personally. Instead, see the value of what your partner is doing for you. He or she is keeping your feet on the ground as you reach for the stars.

Since both of you are relatively unscheduled, your relationship may be able to benefit from a little more planning. This does not mean getting detailed with an elaborate schedule or anything along those lines, but just remember that since you are both in this same subjective camp, you may benefit from an objective influence. For example, if you dream up a great idea that involves moving your family across the country or even across town, you may both get excited about it, but that dream will fizzle out if a concrete plan doesn't emerge. And your accommodating spouse can take only so many exciting dreams that go nowhere.

If you are dreaming about a vacation, for example, and share your dream with your spouse, he or she may not immediately join in the fun if you have a history of only dreaming dreams but never executing them with a plan. It's one thing to get excited about a tropical getaway, but it's another to get practical with a budget and a schedule that will permit it.

So consider how you might incorporate reality into your dreams — especially if your spouse can sometimes get perturbed by talk without action. On the other hand, if you are the kind of

Dreamer that jumps from one dream to the next, often drumming up a lot of activity and motion, recognize how this can wear your partner down. He or she is not hardwired to live in the future. Make sure you carve out moments to be fully present and invested in what's going on right here and now. The more you do this for your partner, the more likely it is that your partner will enter your dreams with you.

Things to keep in mind:

- Don't take it personally if you feel like your partner is holding you back from your dreams. This probably has more to do with your perception than with reality.
- Keep in mind that your spouse is hardwired for the present, not the future. So use his or her leaning to keep you grounded.
- Consider ways to incorporate a little more planning into your relationship. This will help you put your dreams into action.
- Affirm your partner's gift for being more present oriented. This can balance your future focus when you get consumed by a dream.

If You're a Dreamer Married to a Planner

"The best way to predict the future," said Alan Kay, "is to invent it." You could have said the same thing. As a couple, you are fully focused on the future together, and this can be a terrific asset. However, you are more unscheduled about your future than your partner. He or she is objective while you are subjective. And this is where you will sometimes find friction between your two time styles.

To maximize your time together, be aware of how your dreaming can sometimes irritate your partner. Why? Because your partner may see your dreaming as impractical. After all, you are not nearly as objective and scheduled as he or she is. You put your energy into dreaming up a scenario or a project or a future without much regard to whether it is practical or even possible. At least this is how your partner is going to see it. So the first step toward minimizing this is to own it. Acknowledge that your style is not as concrete as your partner's. Even poke fun at yourself regarding this to let him or her know that you know it's not always easy to live with.

Next, recognize the immeasurable value your more objective partner brings to your relationship. As you are probably already aware, it's often a Planner that makes a Dreamer's dream a reality. This is a terrific complement to your time style. Don't let it go unnoticed. Affirm it and regularly vocalize your appreciation for him or her. You may even want to recount ways that your partner has helped you realize your dreams.

Also, the two of you can probably benefit from putting a little bit more of your energy into the here and now. More than most couples, you will be tempted to live for "someday," and eventually miss out on too many "todays." Don't let that happen. Today is what your marriage is made of. Give attention to what's happening between you today. Be intentional about it. Consider how you can maximize this very moment in time rather than short-circuiting it by using it only to talk about what will be.

For example, the two of you may be enjoying a lovely moment at dinner when you cut it short because you have a "great idea" that you want to immediately research on the Internet. Whoa! Ease up and savor the moment a bit more. You don't have to sacrifice the present to take full advantage of your future. This may take some discipline for both of you, but it's sure to help you regain moments you've been missing together and maximize what could easily become a marriage that is far too focused on the future.

Things to keep in mind:

- Own the fact that living with a Dreamer can sometimes be challenging. Let your partner know you recognize this.
- Affirm your partner's objectivity. Express to him or her how valuable it is to you and your relationship.
- Consider ways to incorporate being more fully present in your conversations and your times together. Savor moments you may be tempted to cut short.
- Lean into your partner's ability to help you realize your dreams. Don't misread his or her practicality as a drag on your dreams. It's not. It's only a way to make sure they can be realized.

If You're a Dreamer Married to a Processor

When it comes to your two time styles, you're in what is sometimes known as a complementary relationship. Your subjective approach to time complements your partner's objective experience, and vice versa. The same is true when it comes to where each of you puts your energy. You are future oriented, and this complements your partner's present orientation. So on both dimensions of time—how you experience it and where you focus your energy— you are complementary.

Of course, you may be tempted to say you are "opposite" instead of "complementary," and you'd be right. It's another way of saying that your two differing time styles can either work for you or against you. It all depends on your attitude and your understanding.

You can gain ground in your relationship the moment you recognize that your future orientation is a powerful force to your partner. In other words, your dreams and schemes about the future may seem completely foreign to your processing spouse. Your dreams may bowl him or her over on occasion. After all, for a Processor, time is about the present and what's on the schedule. Your dreams disrupt that schedule or ignore it altogether. On top of that, your dreaming pays little respect to the present, since it is consumed by the future. All this to say that your time style as a Dreamer can try the patience of a Processor. So beware. Do what you can to be sensitive to this fact. Acknowledge it and even laugh about it when you can. This will let your partner know you understand and are sensitive to his or her situation.

Next, do everything you can to affirm the time style of your partner. You probably don't do this as much as you think you do. After all, the Processor approach is one that doesn't always make sense to you. And your desire to be spontaneous and spur-of-the-moment can make your partner feel a bit put-upon or even criticized. He or she may feel like the proverbial stick-in-the-mud compared to you. And that can be intimidating to a Processor. So go out of your way to affirm the value your partner brings to your times together. Acknowledge the gift of structure and orderliness that is in your life because of him or her. This will go a long way to helping each of you complement one another's time styles.

Also, work to be a bit more accommodating with your time. In other words, try to savor the here and now more often. Your dreaming about the future can cut short some wonderful moments that your spouse is enjoying in the present. And the same holds true for being a bit more objective. Respect the schedule of your spouse. Realize that it provides as much security to him or her as your dreaming provides excitement for you.

Things to keep in mind:

- Own the fact that living with a Dreamer can sometimes be challenging. Let your partner know you recognize this as you work to be more fully present in your conversations.

- Regularly affirm your partner's objective time style. Express to him or her how valuable it is to you and your relationship.
- Savor moments you may be tempted to cut short. Just because your time isn't taking you closer to your latest dream doesn't mean it's not valuable.
- Your styles can either complement each other, pulling you together as you appreciate them, or pull you apart. The choice is yours.

If You're a Dreamer Married to a Dreamer

Malcolm Forbes once said, "When you cease to dream, you cease to live." If that's true, the two of you, as a couple, have a long life ahead of you. Because of your shared time styles, you've got a double dose of dreams.

As two Dreamers, you are both more unscheduled than scheduled, and you're both squarely focused on the future. This means you're both hardwired to sacrifice the present for the future. And that's your biggest challenge as you manage your time together and work to build a deeper connection.

You see, your marriage is made up of what you have today — right now. And to a Dreamer, that right now is often leveraged for a better tomorrow. There's nothing wrong with that, as long as it's done in moderation. A marriage can't sustain itself entirely on what will someday be. Eventually you have to live in the here and now. Of course, you are already doing this, but not as much as most couples. As two Dreamers your greatest temptation, when it comes to time, is to bank on what will be. The goal, remember, is not just to achieve a dream but to remain connected in the process of achieving it. That's what Brendan Francis was getting at when he said, "The prospect of success in achieving our most cherished dream is not without its terrors. Who is more deprived and alone than the man who has achieved his dream?"

The point is that two Dreamers need to take special care to connect in the present. That's all. And you can do just that. Begin by savoring moments that are happening right now. Today. Take your evening meal as an example. Since neither of you are all that into schedules, your meal may be at different times each evening. Fine. And that may mean that you don't always share your meal together. Not so fine. Cultivate a plan, schedule it if need be, to dine together whenever you can. And linger. That's not always easy for Dreamers. You're both ready to get on to the next thing. But discipline yourselves to let the moment of connection last before you shift gears and move on.

Also, remember that the downfall of many a good Dreamer is to neglect taking action. Some Dreamers are notorious for talking a big talk and that's it. They don't follow through on their imaginings. And since both of you are in the same "dream boat," you don't have a partner who will help you get concrete and execute a scheduled plan. You don't have an Accommodator or a Processor within your relationship to keep you grounded in the present. This means the two of you will need to take special care to make a concrete plan for achieving your important dreams.

Finally, recognize what a rare gift it is that you two share this exciting approach to time. Couples are rarely matched in this way; usually Dreamers are married to another time style. So cherish and celebrate this combination you have.

Things to keep in mind:

- Remember that both of you are hardwired to sacrifice the present for a payoff in the future. This can get the better of you if you aren't careful.

- Savor your moments together. Pay attention to the here and now. Don't let your present be robbed by your future.
- Consider what actions the two of you need to take to realize your shared dreams. Don't just talk, do.
- Celebrate your shared time styles. It's a rare combination and one that can take you far as you share the experience of your dreams.

If You're a Planner Married to an Accommodator

When it comes to your two time styles, you're in what is sometimes known as a complementary relationship. Your objective approach to time complements your partner's subjective experience, and vice versa. The same is true when it comes to where each of you puts your energy. You are future oriented, and this complements your partner's present orientation. So on both dimensions of time—how you experience it and where you focus your energy—you are complementary.

Of course, you may be tempted to say you are "opposite" instead of "complementary," and you'd be right. It's another way of saying that your two differing time styles can either work for you or against you. It all depends on your attitude and your understanding.

As a Planner, you can recoup moments you're missing together in your marriage by taking a break from planning. Such advice sounds profoundly simple, but it holds true. Planners are perpetually motivated by what's next. This means you get a lot accomplished. But it also means you miss out on a lot of opportunities to connect. That's why taking a break from all your planning and hard work can go a long way in solidifying your connection with your spouse. Granted, this is not always easy for a person who is hardwired the way you are, but you can do it. In fact, taking a break from planning simply needs to be a part of your plan! You need to schedule time where you take a rest from planning and simply savor the time you have with your partner.

Next, beware of the way you set yourself up for frustration. Since your spouse is an Accommodator, you are sometimes going to feel annoyed or bothered by the fact that he or she doesn't always "accommodate" your plans. As an Accommodator, your partner relishes the freedom of living without a structured plan on occasion. He or she likes being freewheeling and spontaneous. And truth be told, you can go with the flow yourself, when you decide to. It just needs to be part of your plan.

So how can you cope with this potential frustration? By poking fun at yourself. After all, it is quite humorous. You have to plan your spontaneity, after all. That's okay. Just acknowledge that's the way you operate and have a sense of humor about it. This will go a long way in helping your partner feel understood and appreciated.

Speaking of which, affirming your partner's accommodating style is imperative. Recognize its value to you as a Planner. Let him or her know that you value how much more you are able to live more fully in the present because of them. Let them know how they help you relax. The truth of the matter is that your accommodating spouse is probably helping you live longer because of the influence of his or her more unscheduled pace.

Things to keep in mind:

- Take a break from your planning tendencies whenever you can. You will need to deliberately force yourself to not focus on the future. Make breaks a part of your plan.
- Have a sense of humor about planning your spontaneity. The quicker you are to poke fun at yourself, the sooner you'll be joining your spirits together.

- Compliment and affirm your partner's time style. Point out specific ways that having a subjective and present-oriented spouse benefits you and your relationship.
- Your styles can either complement each other, pulling you together as you appreciate them, or pull you apart. The choice is yours.

If You're a Planner Married to a Processor

As a Planner, you tend to be more scheduled than unscheduled. And so does your spouse. Processors are particularly adept at running their life with a routine that is relatively predictable. But the two of you differ when it comes to where you focus your energy. While you keep a steady eye on the future, your spouse is more focused on the present. Does this impact the time you spend together? You bet.

First of all, you both enjoy having times on the calendar that you can look forward to. This can be a great relational asset. Each of you likes to be able to count on time you've deliberately carved out together. What the two of you may struggle with is spontaneity. Because the two of you tend to lock onto a plan, you may miss out on opportunities that develop more organically. You both may literally forget to stop and smell the roses because you are busy fulfilling your plan and abiding by the objective process. In other words, your schedule may control you rather than you controlling it.

To overcome this potential problem, consider ways that you both can break away from your planned routine on occasion. Deliberately do something off the cuff. For example, if you planned to go out for your routine dinner and a movie date night, change your mind at the last moment and skip the movie for a walk in the park. You get the idea. The point is that couples who simply live in routines eventually

your time-starved marriage

fall into a rut. So do your best to be spontaneous. This may push you outside your comfort zone a bit—and it will do so even more for your Processing spouse—but it will be a good change of pace and a reminder that the point of your time together is to bring you closer together, not to simply check things off your to-do list.

A potential point of friction for you with a processing style is likely to be what you perceive as a lack of excitement about your plans. You may sometimes feel that your spouse is not joining you in crafting your future together. Don't take this personally. And don't read much into it. A Processor is simply hardwired more for the present than the future.

Also, affirm your partner's processing time style. While you are planning for the future, he or she is helping you keep your feet planted in the present. And that's a good thing. After all, the here and now is where your marriage is lived. If you spend all your time planning for tomorrow, you'll never fully live today. And living today is what your partner does a bit better than you. So verbalize your appreciation of this contribution to your relationship. Your partner's style, in this regard, is a terrific complement to yours.

Things to keep in mind:

- Don't allow your schedules to control you. Give yourself permission to be spontaneous. This is good for you, your partner, and your relationship.
- If you feel your spouse is not joining in on your excitement about the future, don't read too much into this. Processors are built for the here and now.
- Compliment and affirm your partner's ability to help you stay a bit more focused on the present. Point out specific ways that having a present-oriented spouse benefits you and your relationship.

- Celebrate the fact that both of you are relatively good at scheduling times that bring you together (both of your styles lean toward this). Don't neglect to use this to your advantage.

If You're a Planner Married to a Dreamer

If your relationship was a time machine, it would be fueled with high octane and only move in one direction—toward the future. As a Planner and a Dreamer, you are both gifted with a vision for what can be. Relative to other couples, neither of you spends much time wallowing in the past, and you have little patience for the present. Not that you don't respect the here and now of your relationship, but you are both pulled into what could be. What might be. You're both eager to see what's around the next corner.

As a result, the two of you can sometimes miss out on the very best times you might have together. You see, two people who are future oriented sometimes neglect the moments they have to enjoy as they are finding their way into the future. But this doesn't have to be. You don't have to allow this subtle saboteur of your time to snare any more of your precious moments. You can guard against this temptation by being deliberate in your pace. As a Planner, you can do this well, when you decide to. You can schedule times to slow down and just be together. This can be a little tougher for some Dreamers, but your spouse will soon see what a programmed sabbatical from focusing on the future can do for your relationship.

This is not to say that the two of you can't go on enjoying your shared vision for exploring the future together. This is a terrific point of connection in your relationship. Just be sure it doesn't consume all of your here and now.

The difference between your two time styles is found in how each of you approaches schedules. Relative to you, your partner is not as structured and objective with time as you are. While you find comfort in having a firm idea of where you're headed and what mileposts you'll see along the way, your partner is content to meander into the future without much regard to schedules. Your partner navigates more by landmarks than by compass or map. Of course, this differing approach from yours can get under your skin on occasion.

So what can you do? First of all, recognize the good that comes from being more subjective with time. See how your partner's more unscheduled approach provides freedom for spontaneity. This adds spice to your relationship. Your partner provides variety to your life. And as Aphra Behn said, "Variety is the soul of pleasure." Your partner makes your life more fun—even when his or her more subjective time style can get under your skin. So admit it. Fess up to the fact that being married to a Dreamer makes your life more interesting.

Also, make sure you regularly affirm your partner's differing style. Too many Planners take good traits for granted. Express to your partner, in concrete terms, how you value him or her as a partner.

Things to keep in mind:

- Recognize that the two of you resonate when you are dreaming and planning your future. This is a terrific gift and a great point of connection.
- Since you are both hardwired to focus on the future, you'll serve your relationship well to give deliberate attention to the here and now.
- When you sometimes feel friction over how you spend your time together, remember that it probably has to do with being scheduled versus unscheduled. One is not better than the other. They just are.

your personal time-style combinations 159

- Compliment and affirm your partner's ability to help you be a bit more unscheduled and spontaneous — to veer from your plan, just for the fun of it.

If You're a Planner Married to a Planner

Shipshape. That's the way you two like to run your life together. You may differ in your approaches on exactly how this is done, but there's no disputing the fact that, relative to other couples, you both have planned what to do and you do what you plan. You enjoy getting your proverbial ducks in a row. You are each more scheduled than unscheduled and more focused on the future than the present. That's what places the two of you in the same camp as Planners.

So when it comes to managing your time together, you are on the same page. You probably have a calendar with scheduled time to spend together. And if you don't, you're planning to. This can be a huge asset to your relationship. While other couples are fumbling to find the time to be together, you two make the time in your schedules.

Is there a downside? Of course. Because both of you are hardwired for focusing on the future, you can tend to put life on hold. You can be so busy with your plans for what's next that you miss out on what's now. As the late Beatle, John Lennon, once said, "Life is what happens to you while you're busy making other plans." And in no marriage would this be more apropos than yours. As you are making plans for your future, your life is happening in the moment. That's a hard pill to swallow for some Planners. After all, Planners are motivated to create their future by planning well. They see tomorrow as better than today. "Someday we'll ..." or "Tomorrow we'll ..." These phrases are probably heard more often in your relationship than in most others.

your time-starved marriage

So what are two Planners to do? First of all, recognize the gift you have. Each of you enjoys giving serious thought to your tomorrows, and this benefits your relationship. This is a powerful tool you share—and a rarity for a husband and wife. Cherish it. "Where no plan is laid, where the disposal of time is surrendered merely to the chance of incidence," said Victor Hugo, "chaos will soon reign." The two of you, compared to many other couples, have little chaos. This is probably evidenced in everything from your bankbook to how you handle holidays. So celebrate your shared time styles.

Next, protect yourself against living only for the future. This will be your greatest temptation when it comes to your time together. Neither of you is particularly adept at stepping out of your planning mode to smell the proverbial roses. But that's exactly what each of you needs to do. From time to time you need to press the pause button on planning and simply *be*. Don't let the future rob you of your present. Guard against it by "planning" not to plan. Carve out time on your shared schedule where you fast from planning. Don't allow yourselves to talk about what's happening next. Instead, reminisce, for example. This is not the natural tendency of a Planner, but it's valuable to your relationship.

Also, recognize that you can benefit from more spontaneity. Two Planners have a tough time veering from the path of their well-laid plans, but doing a few things that disrupt the schedule will keep your relationship fresh and fun.

Things to keep in mind:

- You both share a terrific gift for planning your future. Don't take this shared point of connection for granted.
- Don't let the future rob you of your present. Protect your relationship from being on fast-forward by occasionally reminiscing.

- Because you're both hardwired to focus on the future, you need to give deliberate attention to the here and now.
- Plan to be spontaneous. This would sound crazy to anyone but a Planner, but that's just what will keep your relationship fresh.

If You're a Processor Married to an Accommodator

As a person who experiences time more objectively than subjectively, and focuses energy more on the present than the future, you are a Processor. You enjoy a balanced pace that has a predictable routine much of the time. Your forte is creating an environment that is stable and steady.

Your spouse, as an Accommodator, shares your orientation to the here and now. This has great benefits for the two of you. When you spend time together, you are both generally present. Neither one of you is pulled into the future — at least not as much as many other people — and this allows you to stay focused on what's happening right now, together.

However, your partner experiences time more subjectively than you do. As a Processor, you enjoy a more scheduled approach to your time. Not so with your partner. And this can create some tension at points between the two of you. Why? Because you may become annoyed that your partner isn't as precise and linear as you are when it comes to mapping out your time. In other words, you may feel your partner is interfering with your routine or messing with what you had in mind. And your partner may become a bit disturbed by your scheduling of time together. After all, as an Accommodator, your partner tends to enjoy going more with the flow than you do and may rely more on emotions than the clock for determining how to spend time.

your time-starved marriage

To help you maximize the moments you two enjoy together, let your accommodating spouse know you understand this approach and validate it. In other words, affirm what your partner's time style does for your marriage. It keeps you more relaxed and opportunistic. Without the influence of your partner's time style, you might miss out on great experiences because you are getting too caught up in processing your schedule. So vocalizing your appreciation of your partner's time style is a terrific way to improve your connection and your times together.

Next, protect yourselves by giving a bit more thought to the future. Since both of you are present oriented, you may tend to fall a bit short when it comes to making plans for what's ahead. This can involve everything in your relationship from how you handle money to how, or if, you plan a vacation or even a date night together. Because of your time styles, you will both need to exert a little more effort in this direction.

In addition, since your processing style may come across as "conventional" and maybe even humdrum to your partner on occasion, you might want to experiment with spontaneity. It's okay to divert from your routine on occasion. In all likelihood, your spouse will view this as a gift to him or her. And that can go a long way in improving your moments together.

Things to keep in mind:

- You two share a terrific gift for living in the here and now. Treasure this common approach as a gift to your relationship.
- Don't allow your focus on the present to swallow up all of your future. Exert a little deliberate effort to plan what's ahead by talking about expectations.

- Celebrate your spouse's accommodating time style. Verbally affirm him or her for helping you be more "unscheduled" and relaxed.
- Step out of your routine on occasion. See this as an opportunity to love your partner by "accommodating" his or her unscheduled approach.

If You're a Processor Married to a Dreamer

When it comes to your two time styles, you're in what is sometimes known as a complementary relationship. Your objective approach to time complements your partner's subjective experience, and vice versa. The same is true when it comes to where each of you puts your energy. You are present oriented, and this complements your partner's future orientation. So, on both dimensions of time — how you experience it and where you focus your energy — you are complementary.

Of course, you may be tempted to say you are "opposite" instead of "complementary," and you'd be right. It's another way of saying that your two differing time styles can either work for you or against you. It all depends on your attitude and your understanding.

As a Processor, it may be disconcerting on occasion to see your partner "caught up" in what you perceive as a "dream world." After all, you may very well be the more realistic or at least the more cautious of the two of you. You appreciate your routines and a scheduled approach to living. Your partner, on the other hand, can sometimes miss out on what's happening right now because his or her emphasis is on what's happening next, or what could happen "someday." While this may get under your skin on occasion, you can take great strides in joining your spirits together by learning to appreciate what your Dreamer brings to your marriage. In fact, as you vocalize your

your time-starved marriage

thankfulness to him or her, you will almost immediately feel your tension release. So take some time to consider specific ways that your spouse improves your marriage because of his or her time style. Vocalize your appreciation. Often.

Also, exert a little effort to join your partner in dreaming about your future together. This may go against your grain in some ways. After all, you may feel like you sometimes need to rein your partner in when it comes to dreaming. But this is how your partner is hardwired for time. So give in a little. Talk about your dreams together. You'll soon see that this joins your spirits together.

And when it comes to your partner joining you in your processing style, be patient. Your spouse is not naturally inclined to view time as you do. In fact, he or she may see your style as boring. Don't take this personally. For a Dreamer, processing is a foreign land. But as you learn to understand and appreciate each other's time styles, your partner will eventually see how your processing style can actually help him or her better realize your shared dreams. After all, every Dreamer needs a partner who is objectively grounded in the present to make dreams come true.

Things to keep in mind:

- Express your appreciation of your Dreamer's time style. It may not be how you want to approach time, but you can still validate what it does for your relationship.
- Dream with your partner. Your spouse is probably starving for a conversation where you dream together. Give your partner this gift.
- Recognize what you can do for your partner. As a Processor, you can enable your Dreamer to better realize your dreams together.

- Your styles can either complement each other, pulling you together as you appreciate them, or pull you apart. The choice is yours.

If You're a Processor Married to a Planner

Both of you approach time objectively. You share a desire to be intentionally scheduled, and this can be a terrific asset for your relationship. On the other hand, each of you thinks about time in a different way. You put your energy into the present, while your partner's goes into the future.

This makes your partner a Planner. And this time style can be a great complement to your processing style. Your partner, after all, helps pull you into the future a little more than you might naturally be inclined to do. This stretches you a bit. Just as you stretch your spouse.

So as you work to bring your spirits together on your differing timelines, you will find tremendous benefit to appreciating what your partner does for your relationship. Think about it. A Planner sets you and your relationship up for good experiences down the line. While you are focused on the here and now, your partner is considering what will benefit your relationship in the future. That's a gift. So vocalize your gratitude for it. Express to your partner how much you appreciate his or her time style.

What does affirming and complimenting your partner's time style do for you and your relationship? Plenty. First of all, it will ease any tension you might be experiencing from being married to a person who is hardwired for the future. Since you don't feel the need to plan as much as your partner does, it's inevitable that this inclination will get under your skin. Expressing your appreciation for it is the best remedy for keeping this from happening.

It will also help you to join your partner in making plans together. Sure, you do this already, but once you vocalize your appreciation of his or her time style, you'll feel your hearts join together more deeply as you have conversations about your future together.

As a couple, you will both occasionally need to work to be a little more unscheduled. Since you are each inclined to experience time objectively, your relationship is vulnerable to a lack of spontaneity. Why does this matter? Because spontaneity infuses your marriage with freedom and creativity. It holds the potential for unlocking sentimental impulses. So don't neglect it. You may both need to "plan your spontaneity" until you get the hang of it. That's okay. Do what you can to be a little whimsical on occasion. Your relatively scheduled lives together will thank you for the relief.

Things to keep in mind:

- Express your appreciation of your Planner's time style. Validate what it does for your relationship by saying it out loud to him or her.
- Plan with your partner. Your spouse will greatly appreciate you joining in on the process of looking to the future. This may not be as natural for you as it is for him or her, but do it anyway.
- As a Processor, you can better enable your Planner to move into the present. You help your partner as much as your partner helps you.
- Deliberately work on being more spontaneous. Neither of you is hardwired for this, but your marriage needs it. In all your processing and planning together, don't neglect to be a little whimsical.

If You're a Processor Married to a Processor

"Steady as she goes." That's your marriage motto when it comes to time. Neither of you wants to rock the boat by doing something that isn't part of your normal routine. You and your spouse tend to be more scheduled than unscheduled. Both of you also focus more of your energy in the present than the future. You're both Processors. This means you're both methodical and generally finish what you start. Relative to other couples, you are more punctual and precise with time. All of these attributes can be a terrific asset to your relationship. After all, you're literally on the same page.

However, you do have a challenge or two because of your shared time style. For one thing, your relationship could most likely benefit from being a bit more unscheduled. In other words, if you can help each other to relax your schedules a little, you will probably find that this more subjective and flexible experience affords more shared moments together.

Novelist Virginia Woolf said, "Rigid, the skeleton of habit alone upholds the human frame." That's certainly true for two Processors. Habit is the name of your game. You probably find great comfort in what others might perceive as a "rut." That's fine, as long as that rut doesn't trip you up. When is this likely to happen? When your routine and schedule become more important than your relationship. Of course, you would never see this coming because it wouldn't be deliberate. It's a subtle process, like one day recognizing the hazard of worn-out floorboards on an often-used staircase.

Consider this. Rather than staying on schedule for the mere sake of doing so, your relationship might benefit from being late to something. It's not the end of the world to be late to some things. Of course, you know that in your head, but two Processors can

168   your time-starved marriage

sometimes lose sight of this fact. You may need to be reminded that you can have time work for *you* rather than the other way around. Since neither one of you is particularly adept at going with the flow when it comes to time, this will be a challenge. But you can do it. In fact, you can help each other in this effort, as iron sharpens iron. If one of you is feeling guilty about breaking from the standard routine, the other can encourage and affirm what's taking place.

As you might guess, your relationship can also benefit if you were a little more intentional about your future. When was the last time you dreamed together as a couple? Chances are it's not an activity you do too frequently. And if you think that you do, you might need a reality check. Two Processors are notorious for thinking that they consider their future more than they actually do. Why? Because, like any couple who shares the same time style, they don't have anyone in their relationship to contrast their processing style against. So give future plans some serious thought. What kinds of plans and dreams have you been neglecting? Don't neglect them for long, or your marriage will surely suffer.

The point is not to do something that makes either of you feel uncomfortable. The point is to leverage all you can to join your spirits together. And for two Processors, that means being a tad more pliable with time and a little more intentional about your future.

Things to keep in mind:

- You share a terrific gift of living in the here and now. Don't take it for granted.
- Become more flexible with your schedules. As each of you learns to flex with your calendar and your clock, your relationships will benefit.

- Focus on your future together. What are your dreams for tomorrow? Talk about them. Revisit them. And reminisce as well.
- Help each other work to achieve more balance. You don't have to go it alone. When it comes to time styles, you're in the same boat.

time-style marriage assessment sample report

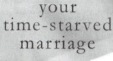

how to stay connected at the speed of life

Time-Starved Assessment
Jane Smith – April 13, 2006

Congratulations on completing the Time-Style Assessment! You now have a tangible picture of how you experience time, and we'll help you use it to stay more connected in your marriage. Of course, to take full advantage of this, you'll want to have your spouse take the assessment as well. So let's begin.

Your Time-Style Grid

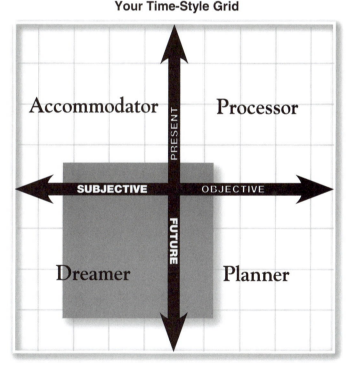

Above is a graphic depiction of where you tend to fall on the four time styles described in the book *Your Time-Starved Marriage*. The shaded box overlaying the quadrants represents your personal approach to time. Notice that it may cover parts of more than one quadrant. Only rarely does anyone fall cleanly and completely into one style. While you may have a general tendency toward one category, your style is likely to incorporate more than just one. However, the quadrant covered most by the shaded box reveals how you generally approach time. This is your "time style."

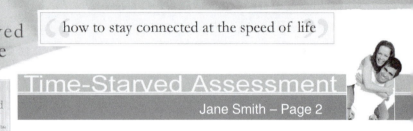

how to stay connected at the speed of life

Making Sense of Your Time Style

The results of your assessment reveal that you approach time as a Dreamer. This means you tend to relate to time more *subjectively* than objectively. In comparison to other people, this makes you more *unscheduled* than scheduled. You're not nearly as "uptight" about staying on task, and you're rarely accused of being regimented.

You are also more oriented toward the *future* than the present. In other words, you love what is about to happen. You have a vision for it. You derive energy from it. And like a visitor from the future, you can tell others (especially your spouse) about the excitement that is just around the bend. No matter that the vision may not be realistic, you want to try it on and simply imagine. You love what could be.

When you are under stress (i.e., your dreams are challenged), you tend to shut down. In other words, you can become immobilized, primarily because your vision for the future is dimming and it isn't as likely to pull you forward. In the same way, you can become a bit unreasonable. When you are stressed, you may be accused of being difficult or irrational. So, on occasion, you have to work at being more realistic and in the here-and-now. Others may think, for example, that you need to be more sensible about what you think can really be done in a certain amount of time. You, on the other hand, are likely to say these people simply haven't caught your vision.

As a Dreamer, you tend to say things like this to your spouse: "I've got a great idea for us" or "You know what we could do instead?" In other words, you may have a moment of inspiration that can instantly change your schedule. You are generally spontaneous and optimistic. Because of this, your approach to time, while not always precise, is often filled with fun and excitement.

Here is a graphic display of your percentages in each of the four time styles.

Your Time-Style Percentages

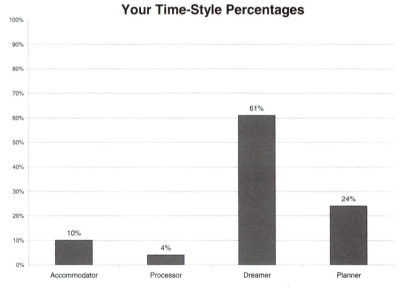

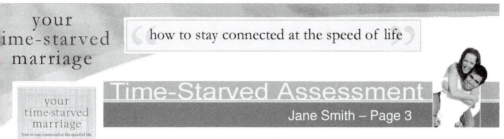

your
ime-starved
marriage

how to stay connected at the speed of life

Time-Starved Assessment

Jane Smith – Page 3

Comparing Your Time Style with Your Partner's

To maximize the results of your time-style summary, we highly recommend that your spouse take the Time-Style Assessment as well. Once you have both taken it, you can compare your time styles and chart a path to more meaningful time together. In fact, the appendix of *Your Time-Starved Marriage* is devoted to helping you maximize the combination of your two time styles.

Read the list below and place a check in the box next to the combination of time styles that describes you:

- ❏ I'm an Accommodator married to a Dreamer
- ❏ I'm an Accommodator married to a Planner
- ❏ I'm an Accommodator married to a Processor
- ❏ I'm an Accommodator married to an Accommodator
- ❏ I'm a Dreamer married to an Accommodator
- ❏ I'm a Dreamer married to a Planner
- ❏ I'm a Dreamer married to a Processor
- ❏ I'm a Dreamer married to a Dreamer
- ❏ I'm a Planner married to an Accommodator
- ❏ I'm a Planner married to a Processor
- ❏ I'm a Planner married to a Dreamer
- ❏ I'm a Planner married to a Planner
- ❏ I'm a Processor married to an Accommodator
- ❏ I'm a Processor married to a Dreamer
- ❏ I'm a Processor married to a Planner
- ❏ I'm a Processor married to a Processor

Now that you have identified your combination of time styles, we encourage you to read the section of *Your Time-Starved Marriage* that applies specifically to your relationship. You will find these descriptions beginning on page 137 of the book.

Try This
You may find it helpful to actually draw a visual replication of your combined styles by using your time-style grid on the first page of this report. Simply examine your spouse's time-style grid (from their assessment) and place it on your grid to see your two styles in relationship to one another.

your
time-starved
marriage

how to stay connected at the speed of life

Time-Starved Assessment

Jane Smith – Page 4

Exploring Your Time Styles Together

As you examine the graphic display and written description of your time style, talk to your spouse about your results. In other words, explore why you think your percentages in these four time styles (Accommodator, Dreamer, Planner, and Processor) are the way the are.

Here are some questions to get you started …

- Do you agree with the percentages of your results—as well as your partner's—in the four time styles? Why or why not?

- How do your two time styles compare with each other? For example, are you in sync when it comes to being "scheduled" versus "unscheduled"? Why or why not? And what are some specific examples of how this can sometimes cause tension between you (whether they are the same or different)? Be specific.

- How do your two time styles compare when it comes to being focused on the present versus the future? Again, be as specific as you can.

- What are some recent examples from your life that demonstrate your dominant time style? Talk to each other about some specific places or times when your two time styles become most apparent.

- What do you see as one of the major assets of your time style? And your partner time style?

- Ask each other: What is most challenging for you when it comes to living with my time style?

- What can you do, in practical terms, to avoid stepping on each other's toes when comes to managing time now that you have a clearer view of your two personal time styles?

Keep This in Mind

The point of this assessment is not to say that you need to approach time differently than you do right now. After all, your time style is, more or less, how you are hardwired for time. The point is to understand your two time styles and how you can maximize them together.

To dig deeper and gain more out of your time-style assessment, consider using one more of the *Time-Starved Marriage* resources located on the following page (if you have done so already). These resources go into greater depth, with practical examples and tool to help you stay connected at the speed of life.

notes

A Quick Overview

1. In case you are wondering why we don't simply include the exercises for you to fill out right here in the book, allow us to give you three reasons. First, providing exercises where you were to write in the book would require that the book be given a different classification in the Library of Congress, thus limiting its accessibility. Second, we have also heard from thousands of grateful readers through the years who appreciate a workbook separate from the main book (as we have done with several other popular titles) so that they can have a more pliable binding and plenty of space to write in a true workbook that becomes their own. And third, a reader need only check the book out of a library if he so desires and can still purchase the workbook for his own use.

Chapter 1: Anybody Have the Time?

1. Stephan Rechtschaffen, *Timeshifting* (New York: Main Street Books, 1997).

Chapter 2: Is Your Marriage Slipping into the Future?

1. "What Moms Say They Need Most," *USA Today*, June 5, 2000.
2. A. R. Hochschild, *The Time Bind: When Work Becomes Home and Home Becomes Work* (New York: Henry Holt and Company, 1997).

Chapter 3: Busyness: The Archenemy of Every Marriage

1. Larry Dossey, *Time and Medicine* (Boston: Shambhala Publications, 1982).

2. Website poll of 1,164 individuals in February 2004, *Marriage Partnership*.
3. Linda Waite and Maggie Gallagher, *The Case for Marriage: Why Married People Are Happier, Healthier, and Better Off Financially* (New York: Broadway, 2001).
4. "Take Back Your Time Day." Posted October 2003. *Office of the Governor. www.michigan.gov.*
5. Bernie Siegel, *Love, Medicine, and Miracles* (San Francisco: Harper & Row, 1986), 172.
6. John Ortberg, *The Life You've Always Wanted* (Grand Rapids, Mich.: Zondervan, 2002), 76.

Chapter 6: Prime Time: Maximizing the Minutes that Matter Most

1. M. Dittmann, *Journal of Family Psychology* 18 (2004): 21.
2. William Doherty, *Take Back Your Marriage: Sticking Together in a World that Pulls Us Apart* (New York: Guilford, 2001).

Chapter 7: Time Bandits: Catching Your Time Stealers Red-handed

1. The effect is named after Bluma Zeigarnik, a Russian psychologist. He first identified the effect in 1927.
2. Doug Ferguson, "A Victory in Clear View," Associated Press, March 11, 2003.
3. Frederick F. Flach, *Choices: Coping Creatively with Personal Change* (New York: J. B. Lippincott, 1977).

Chapter 8: Meals: What's the Rush?

1. Eric Schlosser, *Fast Food Nation* (Boston: Houghton Mifflin, 2001).
2. Robert Putman, *Bowling Alone* (New York: Simon and Schuster, 2000).
3. Carl Honoré, *In Praise of Slowness* (New York: HarperCollins, 2004), 59.

4. As quoted in Honoré, Ibid.
5. Isak Dinesen, *Babette's Feast and Other Anecdotes of Destiny* (New York: Vintage, 1988).

Chapter 9: Finances: Time Is Money

1. Bernice Kanner, "Are You Normal About Money?" *Ladies Home Journal*, October 1998.
2. *U.S. News & World Report*, December 11, 1995.
3. "How Much Money Is Enough," *Fast Company*, July/August 1999, 112.
4. Allen Bluedorn, *The Human Organization of Time: Temporal Realities and Experience* (Stanford, Calif.: Stanford Univ. Press, 2002).
5. Kanner, Ibid.
6. David Bach, *The Automatic Millionaire* (New York: Broadway, 2003). Some people may not have a retirement account, or their employers don't offer a retirement plan. Don't use that as an excuse — open your own individual retirement account. An IRA is a personal retirement plan that anyone who earns income can set up at a bank, brokerage firm, or online. You can make this automatic in fifteen minutes.

Chapter 10: Rest: Recouping What You Crave

1. Diana Burrell, "Working Hard Can Be Hazardous to Your Holidays," *Psychology Today*, July 2001.
2. Families and Work Institute, 2001.
3. Families and Work Institute, 1993.
4. "Leisure Time," *Newsweek*, January 27, 1997.
5. Lee Iacocca and William Novak, *Iacocca: An Autobiography* (New York: Bantam, 1986).
6. *www.mrinetwork.com/press/vacation.htm*
7. Robyn D. Clarke, *Black Enterprise*, December 1, 1999.
8. *The News Letter*, August 31, 2004.
9. Nan Fink, *Stranger in the Midst* (New York: Basic Books, 1997), 47.

10. Christianity has a long tradition of Sabbath observance, so a revitalized Sabbath is more a reclaiming of the Christian birthright than the self-conscious adoption of something Jewish. Jesus observed Shabbat, even as he challenged the specifics of Mosaic Sabbath law, and since at least the year 321, when Constantine declared Sunday as the Sabbath for all his empire, Christians have understood the Sabbath as a day for rest, communal worship, and celebration.

11. As he writes in his letter to the Colossians, "Therefore do not let anyone judge you ... with regard to a religious festival, a New Moon celebration or a Sabbath day. These are a shadow of the things that were to come; the reality, however, is found in Christ" (2:16–17). And Jesus, when rebuked by the Pharisees for plucking grain from a field on Shabbat, criticizes those who would make a fetish of Sabbath observance, insisting that "the Sabbath was made for man, not man for the Sabbath" (Mark 2:27).

12. Judaism speaks of a *neshamah yeteirah*, an extra soul that comes to dwell in you on the Sabbath but departs once the week begins.

13. Henri Nouwen, *The Road to Daybreak* (New York: Image, 1990).

Conclusion: As Time Goes By

1. *www.wd40.com*
2. Herman Hupfeld, "As Time Goes By," Warner Bros., 1931.

Interested in hosting the Parrotts for one of their highly acclaimed seminars? It's easy. Just visit *www.RealRelationships.com* to learn more and complete a speaking request form.

Les and Leslie speak to thousands in dozens of cities annually. They are entertaining, thought-provoking, and immeasurably practical. One minute you'll be laughing and the next you'll sit still in silence as they open your eyes to how you can make your relationship all it's meant to be.

"I've personally benefited from the Parrotts' seminar. You can't afford to miss it."

Gary Smalley

"Les and Leslie's seminars can make the difference between you having winning relationships and disagreeable ones."

Zig Ziglar

"The Parrotts will revolutionize your relationships."

Josh McDowell

"Without a doubt, Les and Leslie are the best at what they do and they will help you become a success where it counts most."

John C. Maxwell

Learn more about the Parrotts' "Becoming Soul Mates Seminar" and their new "Love Talk Seminar."

Click on www.RealRelationships.com
to bring them to your community.

Your Time-Starved Marriage

How to Stay Connected at the Speed of Life

Drs. Les and Leslie Parrott

This is not a book about being more productive —it's a book about being more connected as a couple. In *Your Time-Starved Marriage*, Drs. Les and Leslie Parrott show how you can create a more fulfilling relationship with time—and with each other.

The moments you miss together are gone forever. Irreplaceable. And yet, until now, there has not been a single book for couples on how to better manage and reclaim this priceless resource. The Parrotts show you how to take back the time you've been missing together—and maximize the moments you already have. *Your Time-Starved Marriage* shows you how to

- relate to time in a new way as a couple
- understand the two lies every time-starved couple so easily believes
- slay the "busyness" giant that threatens your relationship
- integrate your time style with a step-by-step approach that helps you make more time together
- stop the "time bandits" that steal your minutes
- maximize mealtime, money time, and leisure time
- reclaim all the free time you've been throwing away

Learn to manage your time together more than it manages you. Dramatically improve your ability to reclaim the moments you've been missing. *Your Time-Starved Marriage* gives you tools to feed your time-starved relationship, allowing you to maximize the moments you have together and enjoy them more.

Hardcover, Jacketed   0-310-24597-4

Also Available:

0-310-81053-1	Time Together	Hardcover, Jacketed
0-310-26885-0	Your Time-Starved Marriage	Audio CD, Unabridged
0-310-27103-7	Your Time-Starved Marriage Groupware DVD	DVD
0-310-27155-X	Your Time-Starved Marriage Workbook for Men	Softcover
0-310-26729-3	Your Time-Starved Marriage Workbook for Women	Softcover

Saving Your Marriage Before It Starts

Seven Questions to Ask Before—and After—You Marry

Drs. Les and Leslie Parrott

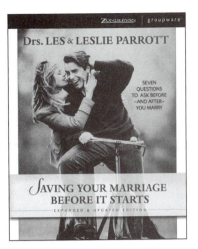

A trusted marriage resource for engaged and newlywed couples is now expanded and updated.

With more than 500,000 copies in print, *Saving Your Marriage Before It Starts* has become the gold standard for helping today's engaged and newlywed couples build a solid foundation for lifelong love. Trusted relationship experts Drs. Les and Leslie Parrott offer seven time-tested questions to help couples debunk the myths of marriage, bridge the gender gap, fight a good fight, and join their spirits for a rock-solid marriage.

This expanded and updated edition of *Saving Your Marriage Before It Starts* has been honed by ten years of feedback, professional experience, research, and insight, making this tried-and-true resource better than ever. Specifically designed to meet the needs of today's couples, this book equips readers for a lifelong marriage before it even starts.

The men's and women's workbooks include self-tests and exercises sure to bring about personal insight and help you apply what you learn. The seven-session DVD features the Parrotts' lively presentation as well as real-life couples, making this a tool you can use "right out of the box." A bonus session for second marriages is also included. The unabridged audio CD is read by the authors.

The Curriculum Kit includes DVD with Leader's Guide, Workbook for Men, Workbook for Women, and hardcover book. All components, except for DVD, are also sold separately.

Curriculum Kit   0-310-27180-0

Also Available:
0-310-26210-0	Saving Your Marriage Before It Starts	Audio CD, Unabridged
0-310-26565-7	Saving Your Marriage Before It Starts Workbook for Men	Softcover
0-310-26564-9	Saving Your Marriage Before It Starts Workbook for Women	Softcover

Love Talk

Speak Each Other's Language Like You Never Have Before

Drs. Les and Leslie Parrott

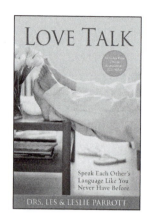

A breakthrough discovery in communication for transforming love relationships.

Over and over, couples consistently name "improved communication" as the greatest need in their relationships. *Love Talk* — by acclaimed relationship experts Drs. Les and Leslie Parrott — is a deep yet simple plan full of new insights that will revolutionize communication in love relationships.

The first steps to improving this single most important factor in any marriage or love relationship are to identify your fear factors and determine your personal communication styles, and then learn how the two of you can best interact. In this no-nonsense book, "psycho-babble" is translated into easy-to-understand language that clearly teaches you what you need to do — and not do — for speaking each other's language like you never have before.

Love Talk includes:

- The Love Talk Indicator, a free personalized online assessment (a $30.00 value) to help you determine your unique talk style
- The Secret to Emotional Connection
- Charts and sample conversations
- The most important conversation you'll ever have
- A short course on Communication 101
- Appendix on Practical Help for the "Silent Partner"

Two softcover "his and hers" workbooks are full of lively exercises and enlightening self-tests that help couples apply what they are learning about communication directly to their relationships.

Hardcover, Jacketed   0-310-24596-6

Also Available:

0-310-80381-0	Just the Two of Us	Hardcover, Jacketed
0-310-26214-3	Love Talk	Audio CD, Abridged
0-310-26467-7	Love Talk	DVD
0-310-81047-7	Love Talk Starters	Mass Market
0-310-26212-7	Love Talk Workbook for Men	Softcover
0-310-26213-5	Love Talk Workbook for Women	Softcover

I Love You More
How Everyday Problems Can Strengthen Your Marriage

Drs. Les and Leslie Parrott

How to make the thorns in your marriage come up roses.

The big and little annoyances in your marriage are actually opportunities to deepen your love for each other. Relationship experts and award-winning authors Les and Leslie Parrott believe that your personal quirks and differences—where you squeeze the toothpaste tube, how you handle money—can actually help draw you together provided you handle them correctly.

Turn your marriage's prickly issues into opportunities to love each other more as you learn how to

- build intimacy while respecting personal space
- tap the power of a positive marriage attitude
- replace boredom with fun, irritability with patience, busyness with time together, debt with a team approach to your finances … and much, much more.

Plus—get an inside look at the very soul of your marriage, and how connecting with God can connect you to each other in ways you never dreamed.

Softcover   0-310-25738-7

Also Available:
0-310-26582-7	I Love You More	DVD
0-310-26275-5	I Love You More Workbook for Men	Softcover
0-310-26276-3	I Love You More Workbook for Women	Softcover

Pick up a copy today at your favorite bookstore!

ZONDERVAN®

GRAND RAPIDS, MICHIGAN 49530 USA

WWW.ZONDERVAN.COM

The Complete Guide to Marriage Mentoring

Connecting Couples to Build Better Marriages

Drs. Les and Leslie Parrott

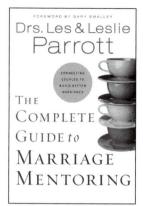

A comprehensive resource to help churches build a thriving marriage mentoring program.

Les and Leslie Parrott are passionate about how marriage mentoring can transform couples, families, and entire congregations. *The Complete Guide to Marriage Mentoring* includes life-changing insights and essential skills for

- Preparing engaged and newlywed couples
- Maximizing marriages from good to great
- Repairing marriages in distress

Practical guidelines help mentors and couples work together as a team, agree on outcomes, and develop skills for the marriage mentoring process. Appendixes offer a wealth of additional resources and tools. An exhaustive resource for marriage mentorship in any church setting, this guide also includes insights from interviews with church leaders and marriage mentors from around the country.

"The time is ripe for marriage mentoring, and this book is exactly what we need."

— Gary Smalley, author of *The DNA of Relationships*

Hardcover, Printed   0-310-27046-4

Also Available:

0-310-27047-2	51 Creative Ideas for Marriage Mentors	Softcover
0-310-27110-X	Complete Resource Kit for Marriage Mentoring, The	Curriculum Kit
0-310-27165-7	Marriage Mentor Training Manual for Husbands	Softcover
0-310-27125-8	Marriage Mentor Training Manual for Wives	Softcover

Pick up a copy today at your favorite bookstore!

ZONDERVAN®

GRAND RAPIDS, MICHIGAN 49530 USA

WWW.ZONDERVAN.COM

The Love List

Eight Little Things That Make a Big Difference in Your Marriage

Drs. Les and Leslie Parrott

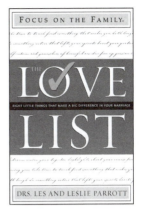

This little book will make a big impact on your marriage. Start right away applying its hands-on concepts, and you'll immediately enjoy more laughter, increase intimacy, gain new direction, and much more.

You'll love how *The Love List* unites purposefulness and spontaneity. "A few small actions—practiced on a daily, weekly, monthly, and yearly basis—can change everything for a couple," say relationship experts Les and Leslie Parrott. "Little, deliberate behaviors quietly lavish love on a marriage."

Discover the importance of tender touch, the bonding power of a clean slate, the secret to building your partner's self-esteem, and the key to putting the sizzle back in sex. *The Love List* isn't so much a to-do list as it is a map for your journey together—one that takes you down the most scenic roads toward meaningful, joyous love and a truly fulfilling marriage. Keep this book handy—and get started today! Includes insert with peel-off his-and-hers "clings" listing the eight items of *The Love List*.

The Love List

Once a Day ...
- Take time to touch (if only for a minute)
- Find something that makes you both laugh

Once a Week ...
- Do something active that lifts your spirits
- Boost your partner's self-esteem

Once a Month ...
- Rid yourselves of harmful residue
- Fire up passion in the bedroom

Once a Year ...
- Review your top-ten highlights
- Chart your course for the coming year

Hardcover, Jacketed   0-310-24850-7

Becoming Soul Mates

Drs. Les and Leslie Parrott

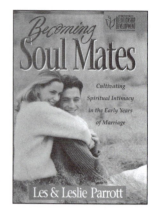

Every couple has a restless aching, not just to know God individually but to experience God together. But how? How do you really allow God to fill the soul of your marriage?

Becoming Soul Mates gives you a road map for cultivating rich spiritual intimacy in your relationship. Written by the creators of the dynamic *Saving Your Marriage Before It Starts* book and program, *Becoming Soul Mates* is a unique and insightful devotional that helps you dig deep for a strong spiritual foundation in your marriage. Fifty-two practical weekly devotions help you and your partner cross the hurdles of marriage to grow closer than you've ever imagined.

In each session you'll find:

- An insightful devotion that focuses on marriage-related topics
- A key passage of Scripture
- Questions that will spark discussions on crucial issues
- Insights from real-life soul mates
- A brief prayer that will help you both draw closer together and close to God

Becoming Soul Mates is a valuable resource for mining the rich potential of your relationship. Its principles, proven in the Parrotts' own relationship, will help you make your journey as a couple all God intends it to be. With the strength that comes from a deeply shared spiritual intimacy, your marriage can flourish in the midst of life's challenges. Start building on the closeness you've got today—and reap the rewards of a deeper, more satisfying relationship in the years ahead.

Hardcover, Jacketed   0-310-20014-8

Also Available
0-310-21926-4   Becoming Soul Mates   Softcover

Pick up a copy today at your favorite bookstore!

ZONDERVAN®

GRAND RAPIDS, MICHIGAN 49530 USA
WWW.ZONDERVAN.COM

You Matter More Than You Think

What a Woman Needs to Know about the Difference She Makes

Dr. Leslie Parrott

Am I making a difference?
Does my life matter?

"How can I make a difference when some days I can't even find my keys?" asks award-winning author Leslie Parrott. "I've never been accused of being methodical, orderly, or linear. So when it came to considering my years on this planet, I did so without a sharpened pencil and a pad of paper. Instead, I walked along Discovery Beach, just a few minutes from our home in Seattle.

"Strange, though. All I seemed to ever bring home from my walks on the beach were little pieces of sea glass. Finding these random pieces eventually became a fixation. And, strangely, with each piece I collected, I felt a sense of calm. What could this mean? What was I to discover from this unintentional collection?"

In this poignant and vulnerable book, Leslie shows you how each hodgepodge piece of your life, no matter how haphazard, represents a part of what you do and who you are. While on the surface, none of these pieces may seem to make a terribly dramatic impact, Leslie will show you how they are your life and how when they are collected into a jar — a loving human heart — they become a treasure.

Hardcover, Jacketed 0-310-24598-2

Pick up a copy today at your favorite bookstore!

ZONDERVAN®

GRAND RAPIDS, MICHIGAN 49530 USA

WWW.ZONDERVAN.COM

We want to hear from you. Please send your comments about this book to us in care of zreview@zondervan.com. Thank you.

ZONDERVAN®

GRAND RAPIDS, MICHIGAN 49530 USA

ZONDERVAN.COM/
AUTHOR**TRACKER**